Edmund Burke

Two Letters Addressed to a Member of the Present Parliament

On the Proposals for Peace with the Regicide Directory of France

Edmund Burke

Two Letters Addressed to a Member of the Present Parliament
On the Proposals for Peace with the Regicide Directory of France

ISBN/EAN: 9783337106980

Printed in Europe, USA, Canada, Australia, Japan

Cover: Foto ©ninafisch / pixelio.de

More available books at **www.hansebooks.com**

TWO LETTERS

'ADDRESSED TO

A MEMBER

OF

THE PRESENT PARLIAMENT,

ON THE PROPOSALS FOR

PEACE

WITH THE

REGICIDE DIRECTORY

OF

FRANCE.

————◦✦◦————

BY THE RIGHT HON. EDMUND BURKE.

————◦✦◦————

London:

PRINTED FOR F. AND C. RIVINGTON,
ST. PAUL'S CHURCH-YARD.

1796.

LETTER I.

On the Overtures of Peace.

MY DEAR SIR,

OUR laſt converſation, though not in the tone of abſolute deſpondency, was far from chearful. We could not eaſily account for ſome unpleaſant appearances. They were repreſented to us as indicating the ſtate of the popular mind; and they were not at all what we ſhould have expected from our old ideas even of the faults and vices of the Engliſh character. The diſaſtrous events, which have followed one upon another in a long unbroken funereal train, moving in a proceſſion, that ſeemed to have no end, theſe were not the principal cauſes of our dejection. We feared more from what threatened to fail within, than what menaced to oppreſs us from abroad. To a people who have once been proud ·and great, and great becauſe they were proud, a change in the national ſpirit is the moſt terrible of all revolutions.

I ſhall not live to behold the unravelling of the intricate plot, which ſaddens and perplexes the

B   awful

awful drama of Providence, now acting on the moral theatre of the world. Whether for thought or for action, I am at the end of my career. You are in the middle of yours. In what part of it's orbit the nation, with which we are carried along, moves at this inftant, it is not eafy to conjecture. It may, perhaps, be far advanced in its aphelion.— But when to return?

Not to lofe ourfelves in the infinite void of the conjectural world, our bufinefs is with what is likely to be affected for the better or the worfe, by the wifdom or weaknefs of our plans. In all fpeculations upon men and human affairs, it is of no fmall moment to diftinguifh things of accident from permanent caufes, and from effects that cannot be altered. It is not every irregularity in our movement that is a total devi-ation from our courfe. I am not quite of the mind of thofe fpeculators, who feem affured, that neceffarily, and by the conftitution of things, all States have the fame periods of infancy, manhood, and decrepitude, that are found in the individuals who compofe them. Parallels of this fort rather furnifh fimilitudes to illuftrate or to adorn, than to fupply analogies from whence to rea-fon. The objects which are attempted to be forced into an analogy are not found in the fame claffes of exiftence. Individuals are phyfical be-ings,

ings, fubject to laws univerfal and invariable. The immediate caufe acting in thefe laws may be obfcure : The general refults are fubjects of certain calculation. But commonwealths are not phyfical but moral effences. They are artificial combinations ; and in their proximate efficient caufe, the arbitrary productions of the human mind. We are not yet acquainted with the laws which neceffarily influence the ftability of that kind of work made by that kind of agent. There is not in the phyfical order (with which they do not appear to hold any affignable connexion) a diftinct caufe by which any of thofe fabricks muft neceffarily grow, flourifh, or decay ; nor, in my opinion, does the moral world produce any thing more determinate on that fubject, than what may ferve as an amufement (liberal indeed, and ingenious, but ftill only an amufement) for fpeculative men. I doubt whether the hiftory of mankind is yet compleat enough, if ever it can be fo, to furnifh grounds for a fure theory on the internal caufes which neceffarily affect the fortune of a State. I am far from denying the operation of fuch caufes : But they are infinitely uncertain, and much more obfcure, and much more difficult to trace, than the foreign caufes that tend to raife, to deprefs, and fometimes to overwhelm a community.

It is often impoffible, in thefe political enquiries, to find any proportion between the apparent force

of

(4)

of any moral caufes we may affign and their known operation. We are therefore obliged to deliver up that operation to mere chance, or more pioufly (perhaps more rationally) to the occafional inter-pofition and irrefiftible hand of the Great Dif-pofer. We have feen States of confiderable duration, which for ages have remained nearly as they have begun, and could hardly be faid to ebb or flow. Some appear to have fpent their vigour at their commencement. Some have blazed out in their glory a little before their extinction. The meri-dian of fome has been the moft fplendid. Others, and they the greateft number, have fluctuated, and experienced at different periods of their exiftence a great variety of fortune. At the very moment when fome of them feemed plunged in unfathom-able abyffes of difgrace and difafter, they have fuddenly emerged. They have begun a new courfe and opened a new reckoning; and even in the depths of their calamity, and on the very ruins of their country, have laid the foundations of a tow-ering and durable greatnefs. All this has happened without any apparent previous change in the ge-neral circumftances which had brought on their diftrefs. The death of a man at a critical junc-ture, his difguft, his retreat, his difgrace, have brought innumerable calamities on a whole na-tion. A common foldier, a child, a girl at the door of an inn, have changed the face of fortune, and almoft of Nature,

Such

Such, and often influenced by fuch caufes, has commonly been the fate of Monarchies of long duration. They have their ebbs and their flows. This has been eminently the fate of the Monarchy of France. There have been times in which no Power has ever been brought fo low. Few have ever flourifhed in greater glory. By turns elevated and depreffed, that Power had been, on the whole, rather on the encreafe; and it continued not only powerful but formidable to the hour of the total ruin of the Monarchy. This fall of the Monarchy was far from being preceded by any exterior fymptoms of decline. The interior were not vifible to every eye; and a thoufand accidents might have prevented the operation of what the moft clear-fighted were not able to difcern, nor the moft provident to divine. A very little time before its dreadful cataftrophe, there was a kind of exterior fplendour in the fituation of the Crown, which ufually adds to Government ftrength and authority at home. The Crown feemed then to have obtained fome of the moft fplendid objects of ftate ambition. None of the Continental Powers of Europe were the enemies of France. They were all, either tacitly difpofed to her, or publickly connected with her; and in thofe who kept the moft aloof, there was little appearance of jealoufy; of animofity there was no appearance at all. The Britifh Nation, her great preponderating rival, fhe had humbled; to

all

all appearance she had weakened; certainly had endangered, by cutting off a very large, and by far the most growing part of her empire. In that it's acmé of human prosperity and greatness, in the high and palmy state of the Monarchy of France, it fell to the ground without a struggle. It fell without any of those vices in the Monarch, which have sometimes been the causes of the fall of kingdoms, but which existed, without any visible effect on the state, in the highest degree in many other Princes; and, far from destroying their power, had only left some slight stains on their character. The financial difficulties were only pretexts and instruments of those who accomplished the ruin of that Monarchy. They were not the causes of it.

Deprived of the old Government, deprived in a manner of all Government, France fallen as a Monarchy, to common speculators might have appeared more likely to be an object of pity or insult, according to the disposition of the circumjacent powers, than to be the scourge and terror of them all: But out of the tomb of the murdered Monarchy in France, has arisen a vast, tremendous, unformed spectre, in a far more terrific guise than any which ever yet have overpowered the imagination, and subdued the fortitude of man. Going straight forward to it's end, unappalled by peril, unchecked by remorse, despising all common maxims and all common means, that hideous phantom

tom overpowerd thofe who could not believe it was poffible fhe could at all exift, except on the principles, which habit rather than nature had perfuaded them were neceffary to their own particular welfare and to their own ordinary modes of action. But the conftitution of any political being, as well as that of any phyfical being, ought to be known, before one can venture to fay what is fit for it's confervation, or what is the proper means of it's power. The poifon of other States is the food of the new Republick. That bankruptcy, the very apprehenfion of which is one of the caufes affigned for the fall of the Monarchy, was the capital on which fhe opened her traffick with the world.

The Republick of Regicide with an annihilated revenue, with defaced manufactures, with a ruined commerce, with an uncultivated and half depopulated country, with a difcontented, diftreffed, enflaved, and famifhed people, paffing with a rapid, eccentrick, incalculable courfe, from the wildeft anarchy to the fterneft defpotifm, has actually conquered the fineft parts of Europe, has diftreffed, difunited, deranged, and broke to pieces all the reft; and fo fubdued the minds of the rulers in every nation, that hardly any refource prefents itfelf to them, except that of entitling themfelves to a contemptuous mercy by a difplay of their imbecility and meannefs. Even in their greateft military efforts

and

and the greatest display of their fortitude, they seem not to hope, they do not even appear to wish, the extinction of what subsists to their certain ruin. Their ambition is only to be admitted to a more favoured class in the order of servitude under that domineering power.

This seems the temper of the day. At first the French force was too much despised. Now it is too much dreaded. As inconsiderate courage has given way to irrational fear, so it may be hoped, that through the medium of deliberate sober apprehension, we may arrive at steady fortitude. Who knows whether indignation may not succeed to terror, and the revival of high sentiment, spurning away the delusion of a safety purchased at the expence of glory, may not yet drive us to that generous despair, which has often subdued distempers in the State for which no remedy could be found in the wisest councils.

Other great States, having been without any regular certain course of elevation, or decline, we may hope that the British fortune may fluctuate also; because the public mind, which greatly influences that fortune, may have it's changes. We are therefore never authorized to abandon our country to it's fate, or to act or advise as if it had no resource. There is no reason to apprehend, because ordinary

means

means threaten to fail, that no others can spring up. Whilst our heart is whole, it will find means, or make them. The heart of the citizen is a perennial spring of energy to the State. Because the pulse seems to intermit, we must not presume that it will cease instantly to beat. The publick must never be regarded as incurable. I remember in the beginning of what has lately been called the seven years war, that an eloquent writer and ingenious speculator, Dr. Browne, upon some reverses which happened in the beginning of that war, published an elaborate philosophical discourse to prove that the distinguishing features of the people of England had been totally changed, and that a frivolous effeminacy was become the national character. Nothing could be more popular than that work. It was thought a great consolation to us the light people of this country (who were and are light, but who were not and are not effeminate) that we had found the causes of our misfortunes in our vices. Pythagoras could not be more pleased with his leading discovery. But whilst in that splenetick mood we amused ourselves in a four critical speculation, of which we were ourselves the objects, and in which every man lost his particular sense of the publick disgrace in the epidemic nature of the distemper; whilst, as in the Alps *Goitre* kept *Goitre* in countenance; whilst we were thus abandoning ourselves to a direct con-

C   fession

feſſion of our inferiority to France, and whilſt many, very many, were ready to act upon a ſenſe of that inferiority, a few months effected a total change in our variable minds. We emerged from the gulph of that ſpeculative deſpondency; and were buoyed up to the higheſt point of practical vigour. Never did the maſculine ſpirit of England diſplay itſelf with more energy, nor ever did it's genius ſoar with a prouder pre-eminence over France, than at the time when frivolity and effeminacy had been at leaſt tacitly acknowledged as their national character, by the good people of this kingdom.

For one (if they be properly treated) I deſpair neither of the publick fortune nor of the publick mind. There is much to be done undoubtedly, and much to be retrieved. We muſt walk in new ways, or we can never encounter our enemy in his devious march. We are not at an end of our ſtruggle, nor near it. Let us not deceive ourſelves: we are at the beginning of great troubles. I readily acknowledge that the ſtate of publick affairs is infinitely more unpromiſing than at the period I have juſt now alluded to, and the poſition of all the Powers of Europe, in relation to us, and in relation to each other, is more intricate and critical beyond all compariſon. Difficult indeed is our ſituation. In all ſituations of difficulty men will be influenced in the

part

part they take, not only by the reafon of the cafe,
but by the peculiar turn of their own character.
The fame ways to fafety do not prefent themfelves
to all men, nor to the fame men in different tem-
pers. There is a courageous wifdom: there is alfo
a falfe reptile prudence, the refult not of caution
but of fear. Under misfortunes it often happens
that the nerves of the underftanding are fo relaxed,
the preffing peril of the hour fo completely con-
founds all the faculties, that no future danger can
be properly provided for, can be juftly eftimated,
can be fo much as fully feen. The eye of the
mind is dazzled and vanquifhed. An abject diftruft of ourfelves, an extravagant admiration of the
enemy, prefent us with no hope but in a compromife with his pride, by a fubmiffion to his will.
This fhort plan of policy is the only counfel which
will obtain a hearing. We plunge into a dark
gulph with all the rafh precipitation of fear. The
nature of courage is, without a queftion, to be con-
verfant with danger; but in the palpable night of
their terrors, men under confternation fuppofe, not
that it is the danger, which, by a fure inftinct,
calls out the courage to refift it, but that it is the
courage which produces the danger. They therefore
feek for a refuge from their fears in the fears themfelves, and confider a temporizing meannefs as the
only fource of fafety.

The

The rules and definitions of prudence can rarely
be exact; never univerfal. I do not deny that in
fmall truckling ftates a timely compromife with
power has often been the means, and the only
means, of drawling out their puny exiftence : But
a great ftate is too much envied, too much dreaded,
to find fafety in humiliation. To be fecure, it
muft be refpected. Power, and eminence, and
confideration, are things not to be begged. They
muft be commanded : and they who fupplicate for
mercy from others can never hope for juftice thro'
themfelves. What juftice they are to obtain, as
the alms of an enemy, depends upon his character;
and that they ought well to know before they im-
plicitly confide.

Much controverfy there has been in Parliament,
and not a little amongft us out of doors, about the
inftrumental means of this nation towards the
maintenance of her dignity, and the affertion of her
rights. On the moft elaborate and correct detail
of facts, the refult feems to be, that at no time has
the wealth and power of Great Britain been fo confiderable as it is at this very perilous moment. We
have a vaft intereft to preferve, and we poffefs great
means of preferving it : But it is to be remembered
that the artificer may be incumbered by his tools,
and that refources may be among impediments.
If wealth is the obedient and laborious flave of
virtue

virtue and of publick honour, then wealth is in it's place, and has it's ufe : But if this order is changed, and honor is to be facrificed to the confervation of riches, riches which have neither eyes nor hands, nor any thing truly vital in them, cannot long furvive the being of their vivifying powers, their legitimate mafters, and their potent protectors. If we command our wealth, we fhall be rich and free : If our wealth commands us, we are poor indeed. We are bought by the enemy with the treafure from our own coffers. Too great a fenfe of the value of a fubordinate intereft may be the very fource of it's danger, as well as the certain ruin of interefts of a fuperiour order. Often has a man loft his all becaufe he would not fubmit to hazard all in defending it. A difplay of our wealth before robbers is not the way to reftrain their boldnefs, or to leffen their rapacity. This difplay is made, I know, to perfuade the people of England that thereby we fhall awe the enemy, and improve the terms of our capitulation : it is made, not that we fhould fight with more animation, but that we fhould fupplicate with better hopes. We are miftaken. We have an enemy to deal with who never regarded our conteft as a meafuring and weighing of purfes. He is the Gaul that puts his *fword* into the fcale. He is more tempted with our wealth as booty, than terrified with it as power. But let us be rich or poor, let us be either in what
proportion

proportion we may, nature is falfe or this is true, that where the effential publick force, (of which money is but a part,) is in any degree upon a par in a conflict between nations, that ftate which is re-folved to hazard it's exiftence rather than to aban-don it's objects, muft have an infinite advantage over that which is refolved to yield rather than to carry it's refiftance beyond a certain point. Hu-manly fpeaking, that people which bounds it's ef-forts only with it's being, muft give the law to that nation which will not pufh it's oppofition beyond its convenience.

If we look to nothing but our domeftick condi-tion, the ftate of the nation is full even to plethory; but if we imagine that this country can long main-tain it's blood and it's food, as disjoined from the community of mankind, fuch an opinion does not deferve refutation as abfurd, but pity as infane.

I do not know that fuch an improvident and ftupid felfifhnefs, deferves the difcuffion, which, perhaps, I may beftow upon it hereafter. We can-not arrange with our enemy in the prefent conjunc-ture, without abandoning the intereft of mankind. If we look only to our own petty peculium in the war, we have had fome advantages; advantages ambiguous in their nature, and dearly bought. We have not in the flighteft degree, impaired the
                                                                strength

ftrength of the common enemy, in any one of thofe points in which his particular force confifts ; at the fame time that new enemies to ourfelves, new allies to the Regicide Republick, have been made out of the wrecks and fragments of the general confederacy. So far as to the felfifh part. As compofing a part of the community of Europe, and interefted in it's fate, it is not eafy to conceive a ftate of things more doubtful and perplexing. When Louis the XIVth had made himfelf mafter of one of the largeft and moft important provinces of Spain ; when he had in a manner over-run Lombardy, and was thundering at the gates of Turin ; when he had maftered almoft all Germany on this fide the Rhine ; when he was on the point of ruining the auguft fabrick of the Empire ; when with the Elector of Bavaria in his alliance, hardly any thing interpofed between him and Vienna ; when the Turk hung with a mighty force over the Empire on the other fide ; I do not know, that in the beginning of 1704 (that is in the third year of the renovated war with Louis the XIV) the ftate of Europe was fo truly alarming. To England it certainly was not. Holland (and Holland is a matter to England of value ineftimable) was then powerful, was then independant, and though greatly endangered, was then full of energy and fpirit. But the great refource of Europe was in England : Not in a fort of England detached

from

from the reft of the world, and amufing herfelf
with the puppet fhew of a naval power, (it can be
no better, whilft all the fources of that power, and
of every fort of power, are precarious) but in that
fort of England, who confidered herfelf as embo-
·died with Europe ; but in that fort of England,
who, fympathetick with the adverfity or the happinefs of mankind, felt that nothing in human affairs was foreign to her. We may confider it as
a fure axiom that, as on the one hand no confederacy of the leaft effect or duration can exift
againft France, of which England is not only a
part, but the head, fo neither can England pretend to cope with France but as connected with
the body of Chriftendom:

Our account of the war, *as a war of communion*,
to the very point in which we began to throw out
lures, oglings, and glances for peace, was a war
of difafter and of little elfe. The independant
advantages obtained by us at the beginning of the
war, and which were made at the expence of that
common caufe, if they deceive us about our
largeft and our fureft intereft, are to be reckoned
amongft our heavieft loffes.

The allies, and Great Britain amongft the reft,
(and perhaps amongft the foremoft) have been mi-
ferably deluded by this great fundamental error;
that

that it was in our power to make peace with this
monfter of a State, whenever we chofe to forget
the crimes that made it great, and the defigns
that made it formidable. People imagined ·that
their ceafing to refift was the fure way to be fecure. This " pale caft of thought ficklied over
all their enterprizes and turned all their politicks
awry." They could not, or rather they would not
read, in the moft unequivocal declarations of the enemy, and in his uniform conduct, that more fafety was to be found in the moft arduous war, than
in the friendfhip of that kind of being. It's hoftile
amity can be obtained on no terms that do not imply an inability hereafter to refift it's defigns. This
great prolific error (I mean that peace was always
in our power) has been the caufe that rendered the
allies indifferent about the *direction* of the war ;
and perfuaded them that they might always rifque
a choice, and even a change in it's objects. They
feldom improved any advantage; hoping that the
enemy, affected by it, would make a proffer of
peace. Hence it was, that all their early victories have been followed almoft immediately
with the ufual effects of a defeat; whilft all
the advantages obtained by the Regicides, have
been followed by the confequences that were natural. The difcomfitures, which the Republick
of Affaffins has fuffered, have uniformly called
forth new exertions, which not only repaired old

D

loffes

losses, but prepared new conquests. The losses of the allies, on the contrary, (no provision having been made on the speculation of such an event) have been followed by desertion, by dismay, by disunion, by a dereliction of their policy, by a flight from their principles, by an admiration of the enemy, by mutual accusations, by a distrust in every member of the alliance of it's fellow, of it's cause, it's power, and it's courage.

Great difficulties in consequence of our erroneous policy, as I have said, press upon every side of us. Far from desiring to conceal or even to palliate the evil in the representation, I wish to lay it down as my foundation, that never greater existed. In a moment when sudden panick is apprehended, it may be wise, for a while to conceal some great publick disaster, or to reveal it by degrees, until the minds of the people have time to be re-collected, that their understanding may have leisure to rally, and that more steady councils may prevent their doing something desperate under the first impressions of rage or terror. But with regard to a *general* state of things, growing out of events and causes already known in the gross, there is no piety in the fraud that covers it's true nature ; because nothing but erroneous resolutions can be the result of false representations. Those measures which in common distress might be available, in greater,

are

are no better than playing with the evil. That
the effort may bear a proportion to the exigence,
it is fit it fhould be known; known in it's quality, in
it's extent, and in all the circumftances which attend it. Great reverfes of fortune, there have been,
and great embarraffments in council: a princi-
pled Regicide enemy poffeffed of the moft important
part of Europe and ftruggling for the reft : within
ourfelves a total relaxation of all authority, whilft
a cry is raifed againft it, as if it were the moft ferocious of all defpotifm : a worfe phænomenon ;—our
government difowned by the moft efficient member
of it's tribunals; ill fupported by any of their conftituent parts; and the higheft tribunal of all (from caufes
not for our prefent purpofe to examine) deprived of
all that dignity and all that efficiency which might
enforce, or regulate, or if the cafe required it, might
fupply the want of every other court. Public profecutions are become little better than fchools for
treafon; of no ufe but to improve the dexterity of criminals in the myftery of evafion; or to fhew with what
compleat impunity men may confpire againft the
Commonwealth; with what fafety affaffins may attempt it's awful head. Every thing is fecure, except what the laws have made facred ; every thing
is tamenefs and languor that is not fury and faction. Whilft the, diftempers of a relaxed fibre
prognofticate and prepare all the morbid force of
convulfion in the body of the State, the fteadinefs

of the phyfician is overpowered by the very afpect
of the difeafe.* The doctor of the Conftitution, pre
tending to under-rate what he is not able to contend
with, fhrinks from his own operation. He doubts
and queftions the falutary but critical terrors of the
cautery and the knife. He takes a poor credit
even from his defeat; and covers impotence under the mafk of lenity. He praifes the moderation
of the laws, as, in his hands, he fees them baffled and defpifed. Is all this, becaufe in our day
the ftatutes of the kingdom are not engroffed in
as firm a character, and imprinted in as black and
legible a type as ever? No! the law is a clear,
but it is a dead letter. Dead and putrid, it is
infufficient to fave the State, but potent to infect,
and to kill. Living law, full of reafon, and of
equity and juftice, (as it is, or it fhould not
exift) ought to be fevere and awful too; or the
words of menace, whether written on the parch-
ment roll of England, or cut into the brazen ta-
blet of Rome, will excite nothing but contempt.
How comes it, that in all the State profecutions of
magnitude, from the Revolution to within thefe
two or three years, the Crown has fcarcely ever
retired difgraced and defeated from it's Courts?
Whence this alarming change? By a connexion eafily felt, and not impoffible to be traced to it's caufe,
all the parts of the State have their correfpon-

* " Muffabat tacito medicina timore."

dence

dence and confent. They who bow to the enemy abroad will not be of power to fubdue the confpirator at home. It is impoffible not to obferve, that in proportion as we approximate to the poifonous jaws of anarchy, the fafcination grows irrefiftible. In proportion as we are attracted towards the focus of illegality, irreligion, and defperate enterprize, all the venomous and blighting infects of the State are awakened into life. The promife of the year is blafted, and fhrivelled, and burned up before them. Our moft falutary and moft beautiful inftitutions yield nothing but duft and fmut : the harveft of our law is no more than ftubble. It is in the nature of thefe eruptive difcafes in the State to fink in by fits and re-appear. But the fuel of the malady remains; and in my opinion is not in the fmalleft degree mitigated in it's malignity, though it waits the favourable moment of a freer communication with the fource of Regicide to exert and to encreafe it's force.

Is it that the people are changed, that the Commonwealth cannot be protected by its laws? I hardly think it. On the contrary, I conceive, that thefe things happen becaufe men are not changed, but remain always what they always were; they remain what the bulk of us muft ever be, when abandoned to our vulgar propenfities, without guide, leader or controul: That is, made to be full of a blind elevation in profperity;

profperity; to defpife untried dangers; to be overpowered with unexpected reverfes; to find no clue
in a labyrinth of difficulties; to get out of a prefent inconvenience with any rifque of future ruin;
to follow and to bow to fortune; to admire fuc-
cefsful though wicked enterprize, and to imitate
what we admire; to contemn the government
which announces danger from facrilege and regicide, whilft they are only in their infancy and their
ftruggle, but which finds nothing that can alarm in
their adult ftate and in the power and triumph of
thofe deftructive principles. In a mafs we cannot
be left to ourfelves. We muft have leaders. If none
will undertake to lead us right, we fhall find guides
who will contrive to conduct us to fhame and ruin.

· We are in a war of a *peculiar* nature. It is not
with an ordinary community, which is hoftile or
friendly as paffion or as intereft may veer about;
not with a State which makes war through wan-
tonnefs, and abandons it through laffitude. We are
at war with a fyftem, which, by it's effence, is inimi-
cal to all other Governments, and which makes
peace or war, as peace and war may beft contribute
to their fubverfion. It is with an *armed doctrine*,
that we are at war. It has, by it's effence, a faction
of opinion, and of intereft, and of enthufiafm, in
every country. To us it is a Coloffus which be-
ftrides our channel. It has one foot on a foreign
fhore,

shore, the other upon the British soil. Thus advantaged if it can at all exist, it must finally prevail. Nothing can so compleatly ruin any of the old Governments, ours in particular, as the acknowledgment, directly or by implication, of any kind of superiority in this new power. This acknowledgment we make, if in a bad or doubtful situation of our affairs, we solicit peace ; or if we yield to the modes of new humiliation, in which alone she is content to give us an hearing. By that means the terms cannot be of our choosing; no, not in any part.

 · It is laid in the unalterable constitution of things:—None can aspire to act greatly, but those who are of force greatly to suffer. They who make their arrangements in the first run of misadventure, and in a temper of mind the common fruit of disappointment and dismay, put a seal on their calamities. To their power they take a security against any favours which they might hope from the usual inconstancy of fortune. I am therefore, my dear friend, invariably of your opinion (though full of respect for those who think differently) that neither the time chosen for it, nor the manner of soliciting a negotiation, were properly considered; even though I had allowed (I hardly shall allow) that with the hord of Regicides we could by any selection of time, or use of means,
· obtain

obtain any thing at all deferving the name of peace.

In one point we are lucky. The Regicide has received our advances with fcorn. We have an enemy, to whofe virtues we can owe nothing; but on this occafion we are infinitely obliged to one of his vices. We owe more to his infolence than to our own precaution. The haughtinefs by which the proud repel us, has this of good in it; that in making us keep our diftance, they muft keep their diftance too. In the prefent cafe, the pride of the Regicide may be our fafety. He has given time for our reafon to operate; and for Britifh dignity to recover from it's furprife. From firft to laft he has rejected all our advances. For as we have gone he has ftill left a way open to our retreat.

There is always an augury to be taken of what a peace is likely to be, from the preliminary fteps that are made to bring it about. We may gather fomething from the time in which the firft over-tures are made; from the quarter whence they come; from the manner in which they are received. Thefe difcover the temper of the parties. If your enemy offers peace in the moment of fuccefs, it indicates that he is fatisfied with fomething. It fhews that there are limits to his ambition or his refentment.

refentment. If he offers nothing under misfortune, it is probable, that it is more painful to him
to abandon the profpect of advantage than to endure calamity. If he rejects folicitation, and will
not give even a nod to the fuppliants for peace,
until a change in the fortune of the war threatens
him with ruin, then I think it evident, that he
wifhes nothing more than to difarm his adverfary
to gain time. Afterwards a queftion arifes, which
of the parties is likely to obtain the greater advantages, by continuing difarmed and by the ufe
of time.

With thefe few plain indications in our minds,
it will not be improper to re-confider the conduct
of the enemy together with our own, from the
day that a queftion of peace has been in agitation.
In confidering this part of the queftion, I do not
proceed on my own hypothefis. I fuppofe, for a
moment, that this body of Regicide, calling itfelf
a Republick, is a politick perfon, with whom
fomething deferving the name of peace may be
made. On that fuppofition, let us examine our
own proceeding. Let us compute the profit it
has brought, and the advantage that it is likely
to bring hereafter. A peace too eagerly fought,
is not always the fooner obtained. The difcovery
of vehement wifhes generally fruftrates their attainment; and your adverfary has gained a great

E   advantage

advantage over you when he finds you impatient
to conclude a treaty. There is in referve, not
only fomething of dignity, but a great deal of
prudence too. A fort of ourage belongs to negotiation as well as to operations of the field. A
negotiator muft often feem willing to hazard the
whole iffue of his treaty, if he wifhes to fecure any
one material point.

The Regicides were the firft to declare war. We
are the firft to fue for peace. In proportion to the
humility and perfeverance we have fhewn in our
addreffes, has been the obftinacy of their arrogance in rejecting our fuit. The patience of their
pride feems to have been worn out with the im-
portunity of our courtfhip. Difgufted as they are
with a conduct fo different from all the fentiments
by which they are themfelves filled, they think to
put an end to our vexatious follicitation by re-
doubling their infults.

It happens frequently, that pride may reject a
public advance, while intereft liftens to a fecret
fuggeftion of advantage. The opportunity has
been afforded. At a very early period in the diplomacy of humiliation, a gentleman was fent on
an errand*, of which, from the motive of it, what-

* Mr. Bird fent to ftate the real fituation of the Duc de
Choifeul.

ever

ever the event might be, we can never be afhamed. Humanity cannot be degraded by humiliation. It is it's very character to fubmit to fuch things. There is a confanguinity between benevolence and humility. They are virtues of the fame flock. Dignity is of as good a race; but it belongs to the family of Fortitude. In the fpirit of that benevolence, we fent a gentleman to befeech the Directory of Regicide, not to be quite fo prodigal as their Republick had been of judicial murder. We folicited them to fpare the lives of fome unhappy perfons of the firft diftinction, whofe fafety at other times could not have been an object of folicitation. They had quitted France on the faith of the declaration of the rights of citizens. They never had been in the fervice of the Regicides, nor at their hands had received any ftipend. The very fyftem and conftitution of government that now prevails, was fettled fubfequent to their emigration. They were under the protection of Great Britain, and in his Majefty's pay and fervice. Not an hoftile invafion, but the difafters of the fea had thrown them upon a fhore, more barbarous and inhofpitable than the inclement ocean under the moft pitilefs of it's ftorms. Here was an opportunity to exprefs a feeling for the miferies of war; and to open fome fort of converfation, which (after our publick overtures had glutted their pride), at a cautious and jealous diftance, might lead to fomething like an

accommo-

accommodation. What was the event ? A ſtrange
uncouth thing, a theatrical figure of the opera, his
head ſhaded with three-coloured plumes, his body
fantaſtically habited, ſtrutted from the back ſcenes,
and after a ſhort ſpeech, in the mock-heroic falſetto
of ſtupid tragedy, delivered the gentleman who
came to make the repreſentation into the cuſtody
of a guard, with directions not to loſe ſight of him
for a moment ; and then ordered him to be ſent
from Paris in two hours.

Here it is impoſſible, that a ſentiment of tender-
neſs ſhould not ſtrike athwart the ſternneſs of politicks, and make us recal to painful memory, the
difference between this inſolent and bloody theatre,
and the temperate, natural majeſty of a civilized
court, where the afflicted family of Aſgill did not
in vain ſolicit the mercy of the higheſt in rank,
and the moſt compaſſionate of the compaſſionate
ſex.

In this intercourſe, at leaſt, there was nothing
to promiſe a great deal of ſucceſs in our future advances. Whilſt the fortune of the field was wholly
with the Regicides, nothing was thought of but to
follow where it led ; and it led to every thing. Not
ſo much as a talk of treaty. Laws were laid down
with arrogance. The moſt moderate politician

in

in their clan * was chofen as the organ, not fo much for prefcribing limits to their claims, as to mark what, for the prefent, they are content to leave to others. They made, not laws, not Conventions, not late poffeffion, but phyfical nature, and political convenience, the fole foundation of their claims. The Rhine, the Mediterranean, and the ocean were the bounds which, for the time, they affigned to the Empire of Regicide. What was the Chamber of Union of Louis the Fourteenth, which aftonifhed and provoked all Europe, compared to this declaration? In truth, with thefe limits, and their principle, they would not have left even the fhadow of liberty or fafety to any nation. This plan of empire was not taken up in the firft intoxication of unexpected fuccefs. You muft recollect, that it was projected, juft as the report has ftated it, from the very firft revolt of the faction againft their Monarchy; and it has been uniformly purfued, as a ftanding maxim of national policy, from that time to this. It is, generally, in the feafon of profperity that men difcover their real temper, principles, and defigns. But this principle fuggefted in their firft ftruggles, fully avowed in their profperity, has, in the moft adverfe ftate of their affairs, been tenacioufly adhered to. The report,

* Boifly d'Anglas.

combined

combined with their conduct, forms an infallible criterion of the views of this Republick.

In their fortune there has been some fluctuation. We are to see how their minds have been affected with a change. Some impreſſion it made on them undoubtedly. It produced some oblique notice of the submiſſions that were made by suppliant nations. The utmoſt they did, was to make some of thoſe cold, formal, general profeſſions of a love of peace which no Power has ever refuſed to make ; becauſe they mean little, and coſt nothing. The firſt paper I have seen (the publication at Hamburgh) making a ſhew of that pacific dispoſition, discovered a rooted animoſity againſt this nation, and an incurable rancour, even more than any one of their hoſtile acts. In this Hamburgh declaration, they chooſe to ſuppoſe, that the war, on the part of England, *is a war of Government, begun and carried on againſt the ſenſe and intereſts of the people*; thus ſowing in their very overtures towards peace, the ſeeds of tumult and ſedition : for they never have abandoned, and never will they abandon, in peace, in war, in treaty, in any ſituation, or for one inſtant, their old ſteady maxim of ſeparating the people from their Government. Let me add—and it is with unfeigned anxiety for the character and credit of Miniſters that I do add—if our Government perſevere,

feveres, in its as uniform courfe, of acting under inftruments with fuch preambles, it pleads
guilty to the charges made by our enemies againft
it, both on it's own part, and on the part of parliament itfeif. The enemy muft fucceed in his
plan for loofening and difconnecting all the internal holdings of the kingdom.

It was not enough, that the Speech from the
Throne in the opening of the feffion in 1795,
threw out oglings and glances of tendernefs. Left
this coquetting fhould feem too cold and ambiguous, without waiting for it's effect, the violent paffion for a relation to the Regicides, produced a direct Meffage from the Crown, and it's confequences
from the two Houfes of Parliament. On the part
of the Regicides thefe declarations could not be
entirely paffed by without notice: but in that
notice they difcovered ftill more clearly the bottom of their character. The offer made to
them by the meffage to Parliament was hinted
at in their anfwer; but in an obfcure and oblique manner as before. They accompanied their
notice of the indications manifefted on our fide,
with every kind of infolent and taunting reflec-
tion. The Regicide Directory, on the day which,
in their gipfey jargon, they call the 5th of Pluviofe,
in return for our advances, charge us with elud-
ing our declarations under " evafive formalities
and

and frivolous pretexts." What thefe pretexts and evafions were, they do not fay, and I have never heard. But they do not reft there. They proceed to charge us, and, as it fhould feem, our allies in the mafs, with direct *perfidy*; they are fo conciliatory in their language as to hint that this perfidious character is not new in our proceedings. However, notwithftanding this our habitual perfidy, they will offer peace " on conditions *as* moderate"—as what? as reafon and as equity require? No! as moderate " as are fuitable to their *national dignity*." National dignity in all treaties I do admit is an important confideration. They have given us an ufeful hint on that fubject : but dignity, hitherto, has belonged to the mode of proceeding, not to the matter of a treaty. Never before has it been mentioned as the ftandard for rating the conditions of peace ; no, never by the moft violent of conquerors. Indemnification is capable of fome eftimate ; dignity has no ftandard. It is impoffible to guefs what acquifitions pride and ambition may think fit for their *dignity*. But left any doubt fhould remain on what they think for their dignity, the Regicides in the next paragraph tell us " that they will have no peace with their " enemies, until they have reduced them to a " ftate, which will put them under an *impoffibility* of " purfuing their wretched projects ;" that is, in plain French or Englifh, until they have accomplifhed

plifhed our utter and irretrievable ruin. This is
their *pacific* language. It flows from their unalterable principle in whatever language they fpeak, or
whatever fteps they take, whether of real war, or
of pretended pacification. They have never, to do
them juftice, been at much trouble in concealing
their intentions. We were as obftinately refolved to think them not in earneft : but I confefs
jefts of this fort, whatever their urbanity may be,
are not much to my tafte.

To this conciliatory and amicable publick communication, our fole anfwer, in effect, is this—
" Citizen Regicides ! whenever *you* find yourfelves
" in the humour, you may have a peace with *us*.
" That is a point you may always command. We
" are conftantly in attendance, and nothing you
" can do fhall hinder us from the renewal of our
" fupplications. You may turn us out at the
" door; but we will jump in at the window."

To thofe, who do not love to contemplate the
fall of human greatnefs, I do not know a more
mortifying fpectacle, than to fee the affembled
majefty of the crowned heads of Europe waiting
as patient fuitors in the anti-chamber of Regicide.
They wait, it feems, until the fanguinary tyrant
Carnot, fhall have fnorted away the fumes of the
indigefted blood of his Sovereign. Then, when

F   funk

funk on the down of ufurped pomp, he fhall have
fufficiently indulged his meditations with what
Monarch he fhall next glut his ravening maw, he
may condefcend to fignify that it his pleafure to be
awake; and that he is at leifure to receive the pro-
pofals of his high and mighty clients for the terms
on which he may refpite the execution of the fen-
tence he has paffed upon them. At the opening
of thofe doors, what a fight it muft be to behold the
plenipotentiaries of royal impotence, in the prece-
dency which they will intrigue to obtain, and which
will be granted to them according to the feniority
of their degradation, fneaking into the Regicide
prefence, and with the reliques of the fmile which
they had dreffed up, for the levee of their mafters,
ftill flickering on their curled lips, prefenting
the faded remains of their courtly graces, to meet
the fcornful, ferocious, fardonic grin of a bloody
ruffian, who, whilft he is receiving their homage,
is meafuring them with his eye, and fitting to their
fize the flider of his Guillotine! Thefe ambaffa-
dors may eafily return as good courtiers as they
went; but can they ever return from that degrading refidence, loyal and faithful fubjects; or with
any true affection to their mafter, or true attachment to the conftitution, religion, or laws of their
country? There is great danger that they who
enter fmiling into this Trophonian Cave, will
come out of it fad and ferious confpirators; and
fuch

fuch will continue as long as they live. They will become true conductors of contagion to every country, which has had the misfortune to fend them to the fource of that electricity. At beft they will become totally indifferent to good and evil, to one inftitution or another. This fpecies of indifference is but too generally diftinguifhable in thofe who have been much employed in foreign Courts; but in the prefent cafe the evil muft be aggravated without meafu,e; for they go from their country, not with the pride of the old character, but in a ftate of the loweft degradation; and what muft happen in their place of refidence can have no effect in raifing them to the level of true dignity, or of chafte felf eftimation, either as men, or as reprefentatives of crowned heads.

Our early proceeding, which has produced thefe returns of affront, appeared to me totally new, without being adapted to the new circumftances of affairs. I have called to my mind the fpeeches and meffages in former times. I find nothing like thefe. You will look in the journals to find whether my memory fails me. Before this time, never was a ground of peace laid, (as it were, in a parliamentary record,) until it had been as good as concluded. This was a wife homage paid to the difcretion of the Crown. It was known how much

a nego-

a negotiation muft fuffer by having any thing in
the train towards it prematurely difclofed. But
when thofe parliamentary declarations were made,
not fo much as a ftep had been taken towards a
negotiation in any mode whatever. The meafure
was an unpleafant and unfeafonable difcovery.

I conceive that another circumftance in that
tranfaction has been as little authorifed by any example; and that it is as little prudent in itfelf;
I mean the formal recognition of the French Republick. Without entering, for the prefent, into
a queftion on the good faith manifefted in that
meafure, or on it's general policy, I doubt, upon
mere temporary confiderations of prudence, whether it was perfectly advifeable. It is not within
the rules of dexterous conduct to make an acknowledgment of a contefted title in your enemy,
before you are morally certain that your recognition will fecure his friendfhip. Otherwife it is a
meafure worfe than thrown away. It adds infinitely to the ftrength, and confequently to the demands of the adverfe party. He has gained a
fundamental point without an equivalent. It has
happened as might have been forefeen. No notice whatever was taken of this recognition. In
fact, the Directory never gave themfelves any concern about it; and they received our acknowledgment with perfect fcorn. With them, it is not for
the

the States of Europe to judge of their title: But in
their eye the title of every other power depends
wholly on their pleafure.

Preliminary declarations of this fort, thrown
out at random, and fown, as it were, broad-caft,
were never to be found in the mode of our proceeding with France and Spain, whilft the great
Monarchies of France and Spain exifted. I do not
fay, that a diplomatick meafure ought to be, like
a parliamentary or a judicial proceeding, according
to ftrict precedent. I hope I am far from that
pedantry: But this I know, that a great ftate
ought to have fome regard to it's antient maxims;
efpecially where they indicate it's dignity; where
they concur with the rules of prudence; and above
all, where the circumftances of the time require
that a fpirit of innovation fhould be refifted, which
leads to the humiliation of fovereign powers. It
would be ridiculous to affert, that thofe powers have
fuffered nothing in their eftimation. I admit, that
the greater interefts of ftate will for a moment
fuperfede all other confiderations: but if there
was a rule that a fovereign never fhould let down his
dignity without a fure payment to his intereft, the
dignity of Kings would be held high enough.
At prefent, however, fafhion governs in more ferious things than furniture and drefs. It looks as
if fovereigns abroad were emulous in bidding
againft

against their eftimation. It feems as if the pre-eminence of Regicide was acknowledged; and that
Kings tacitly ranked themfelves below their facri-
legious murderers, as natural magiftrates and
judges over them. It appears as if dignity were the
prerogative of crime; and a temporifing humiliation
the proper part for venerable authority. If the
vileft of mankind are refolved to be the moft wicked, they lofe all the bafenefs of their origin, and
take their place above Kings. This example in foreign Princes, I truft, will not fpread. It is the
concern of mankind, that the deftruction of order
fhould not be a claim to rank: that crimes fhould
not be the only title to pre-eminence and honour.

At this fecond ftage of humiliation, (I mean
the infulting declaration in confequence of the
meffage to both Houfes of Parliament) it might
not have been amifs to paufe; and not to fquander
away the fund of our fubmiffions, until we know
what final purpofes of publick intereft they might
anfwer. The policy of fubjecting ourfelves to further infults is not to me quite apparent. It was
refolved however, to hazard a third trial. Citizen
Barthelemi had been eftablifhed on the part of the
new Republick, at Bafle; where, with his procon-
fulate of Switzerland and the adjacent parts of Germany, he was appointed as a fort of factor to deal
in the degradation of the crowned heads of Europe.

At

At Bafle it was thought proper, in order to keep others, I fuppofe, in countenance, that Great Britain fhould appear at this market, and bid with the reft, for the mercy of the People-King.

On the 6th of March 1796 Mr. Wickham, in confequence of authority, was defired to found France on her difpofition towards a general pacification; to know whether fhe would confent to fend Minifters to a Congrefs at fuch a place as might be hereafter agreed upon; to know whether they would communicate the general grounds of a pacification fuch as France (the diplomatick name of the Regicide power) would be willing to propofe, as a foundation for a negociation for peace with his Majefty *and his allies:* but he had no authority to enter into any negociation or difcuffion with him upon thefe fubjects.

On the part of Great Britain this meafure was a voluntary act, wholly uncalled for on the part of Regicide. Suits of this fort are at leaft ftrong indications of a defire for accommodation. Any other body of men but the Directory would be fomewhat foothed with fuch advances. They could not however begin their anfwer, which was given without much delay, and communicated on the 28th of the fame month, without a preamble of infult and reproach. " They doubt the fincerity
of

of the pacifick intentions of this Court." She did not begin, fay they, yet to " know her real inte‑ rests," " she did not feek peace *with good faith.*" This, or fomething to this effect, has been the con‑ ftant preliminary obfervation, (now grown into a fort of office-form) on all our overtures to this power : a perpetual charge on the Britifh Govern‑ ment of fraud, evafion, and habitual perfidy.

It might be afked, from whence did thefe opi‑ nions of our infincerity and ill faith arife? It was, becaufe the Britifh Miniftry (leaving to the Direc‑ tory however to propofe a better mode) propofed a *Congrefs* for the purpofe of a general pacification, and this they faid " would render negociation end‑ lefs." From hence they immediately inferred a fraudulent intention in the offer. Unqueftionably their mode of giving the law would bring matters to a more fpeedy conclufion. As to any other me‑ thod more agreeable to them than a Congrefs, an alternative exprefsly propofed to them, they did not condefcend to fignify their pleafure.

This refufal of treating conjointly with the pow‑ ers allied againft this Republick, furnifhes matter for a great deal of ferious reflexion. They have hitherto conftantly declined any other than a treaty with a fingle power. By thus diffociating every State from every other, like deer feparated

from

from the herd, each power is treated with, on the merit of his being a deferter from the common caufe. In that light the Regicide power finding each of them infulated and unprotected, with great facility gives the law to them all. By this fyftem for the prefent, an incurable diftruft is fown among't confederates; and in future all alliance is rendered impracticable. It is thus they have treated with Pruffia, with Spain, with Sardinia, with Bavaria, with the Ecclefiaftical State, with Saxony; and here we fee them refufe to treat with Great Britain in any other mode. They muft be worfe than blind who do not fee with what undeviating regularity of fyftem, in this cafe and in all cafes, they purfue their fcheme for the utter deftruction of every independent power; efpecially the fmaller, who cannot find any refuge whatever but in fome common caufe.

Renewing their taunts and reflections, they tell Mr. Wickham, " that their policy has no guides " but opennefs and good faith, and that their " conduct fhall be conformable to thefe princi- " ples." They fay concerning their Government, that " yielding to the ardent defire by which it is " animated to procure peace for the French Re- " publick, and for all nations, it will not *fear to* " *declare itfelf openly.* Charged by the Conftitu- " tion with the execution of the *laws*, it cannot

G   *make*

" *make* or *liſten* to any propoſal that would be
" contrary to them. The conſtitutional act does
" not permit it to conſent to any alienation of
" that which, according to the exiſting laws, con-
" ſtitutes the territory of the Republick."

" With reſpect to the countries *occupied by the*
" *French armies and which have not been united to*
" *France*, they, as well as other intereſts political
" and commercial, may become the ſubject of a
" negociation, which will preſent to the Directory
" the means of proving how much it deſires to
" attain ſpeedily to a happy pacification. That
" the Directory is ready to receive in this reſpect
" any overtures that ſhall be juſt, reaſonable, and
" compatible *with the dignity of the Republick.*"
On the head of what is *not* to be the ſubject of
negotiation, the Directory is clear and open. As
to what may be a matter of treaty, all this open
dealing is gone. She retires into her ſhell. There
ſhe expects overtures from *you*—and that you are
to gueſs what ſhe ſhall judge juſt, reaſonable, and
above all, *compatible with her dignity.*

In the records of pride there does not exiſt ſo
inſulting a declaration. It is inſolent in words,
in manner, but in ſubſtance it is not only inſulting
but alarming. It is a ſpecimen of what may be
expected from the maſters we are preparing for
our

our humbled country. Their opennefs and can-
dour confift in a direct avowal of their defpotifm
and ambition. We know that their declared refolution had been to furrender no object belonging to
France previous to the war. They had refolved,
that the Republick was entire, and muft remain fo.
As to what fhe has conquered from the allies and
united to the fame indivifible body, it is of
the fame nature. That is, the allies are to give
up whatever conquefts they have made or may
make upon France, but all which fhe has violently ravifhed from her neighbours and thought
fit to appropriate. are not to become fo much as
objects of negociation.

In this unity and indivifibility of poffeffion are
funk ten immenfe and wealthy provinces, full of
ftrong, flourifhing and opulent cities, the Auftrian
Netherlands, the part of Europe the moft neceffary
to preferve any communication between this kingdom and its natural allies, next to Holland the
moft int refting to this country, and without
which Holland muft virtually belong to France.
Savoy and Nice, the keys of Italy, and the cita-
del in her hands to bridle Switzerland, are in
that confolidation. The important territory of
Leige is torn out of the heart of the Empire. All
thefe are integrant parts of the Republick; not to
be fubject to any difcuffion, or to be purchafed

by any equivalent. Why ? becaufe there is a law which prevents it. What law? The law of nations? The acknowledged public law of Europe? Treaties and conventions of parties? No! not a pretence of the kind. It is a declaration not made in confe-quence of any prefcription on her fide, not on any ceffion or dereliction, actual or tacit, of other pow-ers. It is a declaration *pendente lite* in the middle of a war, one principal object of which was origi-nally the defence, and has fince been the recovery of thefe very countries.

This ftrange law is not made for a trivial object, not for a fingle port, or for a fingle fortrefs; but for a great kingdom; for the religion, the morals, the laws, the liberties, the lives and fortunes of millions of human creatures, who without their confent, or that of their lawful government, are, by an arbitrary act of this regicide and homicide Government, which they call a law, incorporated into their tyranny.

In other words, their will is the law, not only at home, but as to the concerns of every na-tion. Who has made that law but the Regicide Republick itfelf, whofe laws, like thofe of the Medes and Perfians, they cannot alter or abrogate, or even fo much as take into confideration ? With-out the leaft ceremony or compliment, they have
sent

fent out of the world whole fets of laws and law-givers. They have fwept away the very conftitutions under which the Legiflatures acted, and the Laws were made. Even the fundamental facred rights of man they have not fcrupled to profane. They have fet this holy code at nought with ignominy and fcorn. Thus they treat all their domeftick laws and conftitutions, and even what they had confidered as a Law of Nature ; but whatever they have put their feal on for the purpofes of their ambition, and the ruin of their neighbours, this alone is invulnerable, impaffible, immortal. Affuming to be mafters of every thing human and divine, here, and here alone, it feems they are limited, " cooped and cabined in;" and this omnipotent legiflature finds itfelf wholly without the power of exercifing it's favourite attribute, the love of peace. In other words, they are powerful to ufurp, impotent to reftore; and equally by their power and their impotence they aggrandize themfelves, and weaken and impoverifh you and all other nations.

Nothing can be more proper or more manly than the ftate publication called a *note* on this proceeding, dated Downing-ftreet, the 10th of April, 1796. Only that it is better expreffed, it perfectly agrees with the opinion I have taken the liberty of fubmitting

submitting to your confideration.* I place it below at full length as my juftification in thinking
that this aftonifhing paper is not only a direct
negative, to all treaty, but is a rejection of every
principle upon which treaties could be made. To
admit it for a moment were to erect this power,
ufurped at home, into a Legiflature to govern

---

* " This Court has feen, with regret, how far the tone and
fpirit of that anfwer, the nature and extent of the demands
which it contains, and the manner of announcing them, are
remote from any difpofitions for peace.

" The inadmiffible pretenfion is there avowed of appropri-
ating to France all that the laws exifting there may have com-
prifed under the denomination of French territory. To a demand fuch as this, is added an exprefs declaration that no pro-
pofal contrary to it will be made, or even liftened to And
even this, under the pretence of an internal regulation, the
provifions of which are wholly foreign to all other nations.

" While thefe difpofitions fhall be perfifted in, nothing is
left for the King, but to profecute a war equally juft and neceffary.

" Whenever his enemies fhall manifeft more pacific fentiments, his Majefty will, at all times, be eager to concur in
them, by lending himfelf, in concert with his allies, to all
fuch meafures as fhall be calculated to re-eftablifh general tranquillity on conditions juft, honourable and permanent, either
by the eftablifhment of a general Congrefs, which has been fo
happily the means of reftoring peace to Europe, or by a preliminary difcuffion of the principles which may be propofed, on
either fide, as a foundation of a general pacification ; or, laftly,
by an impartial examination of any other way which may be
pointed out to him for arriving at the fame falutary end."

Downing-Street, April 10, 1796.

mankind.

mankind. It is an authority that on a thoufand oc-
cafions they have afferted in claim, and whenever
they are able, exerted in practice. The dereliction
of this whole fcheme of policy became, therefore,
an indifpenfible previous condition to all renewal
of treaty. The remark of the Britifh Cabinet on
this arrogant and tyrannical claim is natural and
unavoidable. Our Miniftry ftate, " *That while thefe
difpofitions fhall be perfifted in, nothing is left for the
King but to profecute a war that is juft and neceffary.*"

It was of courfe, that we fhould wait until the
enemy fhewed fome fort of difpofition on their
part to fulfil this condition. It was hoped indeed that our fuppliant ftrains might be fuffered
to fteal into the auguft ear in a more propitious
feafon. That feafon, however, invoked by fo many
vows, conjurations and prayers, did not come.
Every declaration of hoftility renovated, and every
act purfued with double animofity—the over-run-
ning of Lombardy—the fubjugation of Piedmont—
the poffeffion of its impregnable fortreffes—the
feizing on all the neutral ftates of Italy—our expulfion from Leghorn—inftances for ever renewed for
our expulfion from Genoa—Spain rendered fubject
to them and hoftile to us—Portugal bent under the
yoke—half the Empire over-run and ravaged, were
the only figns which this mild Republick thought
proper to manifeft of their pacific fentiments.
Every

Every demonstration of an implacable rancour and an untameable pride were the only encouragements we received to the renewal of our supplications. Here therefore they and we were fixed. Nothing was left to the British Ministry but " to prosecute a war just and necessary"—a war equally just as at the time of our engaging in it—a war become ten times more necessary by every thing which happened afterwards. This resolution was soon, however, forgot. It felt the heat of the season and melted away. New hopes were entertained from supplication. No expectations, indeed, were then formed from renewing a direct application to the French Regicides through the Agent General for the humiliation of Sovereigns. At length a step was taken in degradation which even went lower than all the rest. Deficient in merits of our own, a Mediator was to be sought—and we looked for that Mediator at Berlin ! The King of Prussia's merits in abandoning the general cause might have obtained for him some sort of influence in favour of those whom he had deserted—but I have never heard that his Prussian Majesty had lately disco-vered so marked an affection for the Court of St. James's, or for the Court of Vienna, as to excite much hope of his interposing a very powerful me-diation to deliver them from the distresses into which he had brought them.

If

If humiliation is the element in which we live, if it is become not only our occafional policy but our habit, no great objection can be made to the modes in which it may be diverfified; though, I confefs, I cannot be charmed with the idea of our expofing our lazar fores at the door of every proud fervitor of the French Republick, where the court-dogs will not deign to lick them. We had, if I am not miftaken, a minifter at that court, who might try it's temper, and recede and advance as he found backwardnefs or encouragement. But to fend a gentleman there on no other errand than this, and with no affurance whatever that he fhould not find, what he did find, a repulfe, feems to me to go far beyond all the demands of a humiliation merely politick. I hope, it did not arife from a predeliction for that mode of conduct.

The cup of bitternefs was not, however, drained to the dregs. Bafle and Berlin were not fufficient. After fo many and fo diverfified repulfes, we were refolved to make another trial, and to try another Mediator, among the unhappy gentlemen in whofe perfons Royalty is infulted and degraded at the feat of plebeian pride, and upftart infolence.—— There is a minifter from Denmark at Paris. Without any previous encouragement to that; any more than the other fteps, we fent through this

H   turnpike

turnpike to demand a paffport for a perfon who on our part was to folicit peace in the metropolis, at the footftool of Regicide itfelf. It was not to be expected that any one of thofe degraded beings could have influence enough to fettle any part of the terms in favour of the candidates for further degradation ; befides, fuch intervention would be a direct breach in their fyftem, which did not permit one fovereign power to utter a word in the concerns of his equal.—Another repulfe.—We were defired to apply directly in our perfons.— We fubmitted and made the application.

It might be thought that here, at length, we had touched the bottom of humiliation ; our lead was brought up covered with mud. But " in the " loweft deep, a lower deep" was to open for us ftill more profound abyffes of difgrace and fhame. However, in we leaped. We came forward in our own name. The paffport, fuch a paffport and fafe conduct as would be granted to thieves, who might come in to betray their accomplices, and no better, was granted to Britifh fupplication. To leave no doubt of it's fpirit, as foon as the rumour of this act of condefcenfion could get abroad, it was formally announced with an explanation from authority, containing an invective againft the Miniftry of Great Britain, their habitual frauds, their proverbial, *punick* perfidy. No fuch State Paper, as a
preliminary

preliminary to a negociation for peace has ever yet
appeared. Very few declarations of war have ever
fhewn fo much and fo unqualified animofity. I
place it below * as a diplomatick curiofity: and in
order to be the better underftood, in the few remarks
I have

* *Official Note, extracted from the Journal of the Defenders of the
Country.*
    Executive Directory.

" Different Journals have advanced that an Englifh Pleni-
potentiary had reached Paris, and had prefented himfelf to the
Executive Directory, but that his propofitions not having appeared fatisfactory, he had received orders inftantly to quit
France.

" All thefe affertions are equally falfe.

" The notices given, in the Englifh Papers, of a Minifter
having been fent to Paris, there to treat of peace, bring to re-
collection the overtures of Mr. Wickham to the Ambaffador
of the Republick at Bafle, and the rumours circulated relative
to the miffion of Mr. Hammond to the Court of Pruffia. The
infignificance, or rather the *fubtle duplicity*, the *PUNICK fi'e of*
Mr. Wickham's note, is not forgotten. According to the partizans of the Englifh Miniftry, it was to Paris that Mr. Hammond was to come to fpeak for peace: when his deftination
became publick, and it was known that he went to Pruffia, the
fame writer repeated that it was to accelerate a peace, and notwithftanding the object, now well known, of this negociation,
was to engage Pruffia to break her treaties with the Republick,
and to return into the coalition—The Court of Berlin, faithful
to its engagements, repulfed thefe *perfidious* propofitions. But
in converting this intrigue into a miffion for peace, the Englifh
Miniftry joined to the hope of giving a new enemy to France,
*that of juftifying the continuance of the war in the eyes of the Englifh
nation, and of throwing all the odium of it on the French Government.*

Su·h

I have to make upon a piece which indeed defies all defcription—" None but itfelf can be it's parallel."

I pafs by all the infolence and contumely of the performance as it comes from them. The queftion is not now how we are to be affected with it

Such was alfo the aim of Mr. Wickham's note. *Such is ftill that of the notices given at this time in the Englifh papers.*

" This aim will appear evident, if we reflect how difficult it is, that the ambitious Government of England fhould fincerely wifh for a peace that would *fnatch from it it's maritime preponderancy, would re-eftablifh the freedom of the feas, would give a new impulfe to the Spanifh, Dutch, and French marines,* and would carry to the higheft degree of profperity the induftry and commerce of thofe nations in which it has always found *rivals,* and which it has confidered as *enemies* of it's commerce, when they were tired of being it's *dupes.*

" But there will *no longer be any credit given to the pacific intentions of the Englifh Miniftry, when it is known, that it's gold and it's intrigues, it's open practices, and it's infinuations, befiege more than ever the Cabinet of Vienna, and are one of the principal obftacles to the negociation which* that Cabinet *would of itfelf be induced to enter on for peace.*

" They will no longer *be credited,* finally, when the moment of the rumour of thefe overtures being circulated is confidered. *The Englifh nation fupports impatiently the continuance of the war, a reply muft be made to it's complaints, it's reproaches :* the Parliament is about to re-open it's fittings, the mouths of the orators who will declaim againft the war muft be fhut, the demand of new taxes muft be juftified ; and to obtain thefe refults, it is neceffary to be enabled to advance, that the French Government refufes every reafonable propofition of peace.

in

in regard to our dignity. That is gone. I fhall fay no more about it. Light lie the earth on the afhes of Englifh pride. I fhall only obferve upon it *politically*, and as furnifhing a direction for our own conduct in this low bufinefs.

The very idea of a negociation for peace, what-ever the inward fentiments of the parties may be, implies fome confidence in their faith, fome de-gree of belief in the profeffions which are made concerning it. A temporary and occafional credit, at leaft, is granted. Otherwife men ftumble on the very threfhold. I therefore wifh to afk what hope we can have of their good faith, who, as the very bafis of the negociation, affume the ill faith and treachery of thofe they have to deal with? The terms, as againft us, muft be fuch as imply a full fecurity againft a treacherous conduct—that is what this Directory ftated in it's firft declaration, to place us " in an utter impoffibility of execut-" ing our wretched projects." This is the omen, and the fole omen, under which we have confented to open our treaty.

The fecond obfervation I have to make upon it, (much connected undoubtedly with the firft,) is, that they have informed you of the refult they propofe from the kind of peace they mean to grant you ; that is to fay, the union they propofe among nations

nations with the view, of rivalling our trade and destroying our naval power : and this they suppose (and with good reason too) must be the inevitable effect of their peace. It forms one of their principal grounds for suspecting our Ministers could not be in good earnest in their proposition. They make no scruple beforehand to tell you the whole of what they intend ; and this is what we call, in the modern style, the acceptance of a proposition for peace! In old language it would be called a most haughty, offensive, and insolent rejection of all treaty.

Thirdly, they tell you what they conceive to be the perfidious policy which dictates your delusive offer; that is, the design of cheating not only them, but the people of England, against whose interest and inclination this war is supposed to be carried on.

If we proceed in this business, under this preliminary declaration, it seems to me, that we admit, (now for the third time) by something a great deal stronger than words, the truth of the charges of every kind which they make upon the British Ministry, and the grounds of those foul imputations. The language used by us, which in other circumstances would not be exceptionable, in this case tends very strongly to confirm and realize the suspicion

picion of our enemy. I mean the declaration, that if we do not obtain fuch terms of peace as fuits our opinion of what our interefts require, *then*, and in *that* cafe, we fhall continue the war with vigour. This offer fo reafoned plainly implies, that without it, our leaders themfelves entertain great doubts of the opinion and good affections of the Britifh people; otherwife there does not appear any caufe, why we fhould proceed under the fcandalous conftruction of our enemy, upon the former offer made by Mr. Wickham, and on the new offer made directly at Paris. It is not, therefore, from a fenfe of dignity, but from the danger of radicating that falfe fentiment in the breafts of the enemy, that I think, under the aufpices of this declaration, we cannot, with the leaft hope of a good event, or, indeed, with any regard to the common fafety, proceed in the train of this negociation. I wifh Miniftry would ferioufly confider the importance of their feeming to confirm the enemy in an opinion, that his frequent appeals to the people againft their Government has not been without it's effect. If it puts an end to this war, it will render another impracticable.

Whoever goes to the directorial prefence under this paffport, with this offenfive comment, and foul explanation, goes, in the avowed fenfe of the Court to which he is fent; as the inftrument of a
Government

Government diffociated from the interefts and wifhes of the Nation, for the purpofe of cheating both the people of France and the people of England. He goes out the declared emiffary of a faithlefs Minif-try. He has perfidy for his credentials. He has na-tional weaknefs for his full powers. I yet doubt whether any one can be found to inveft himfelf with that character. If there fhould, it would be pleafant to read his inftructions on the anfwer which he is to give to the Directory, in cafe they fhould repeat to him the fubftance of the Mani-fefto which he carries with him in his portfolio.

So much for the *firft* Manifefto of the Regicide Court which went along with the paffport. Left this declaration fhould feem the effect of hafte, or a mere fudden effufion of pride and infolence, on full deliberation, about a week after comes out a fecond. In this manifefto, which is dated the fifth of October, one day before the fpeech from the Throne, on the vigil of the feftive day of cordial unanimity fo happily celebrated by all parties in the Britifh Par-liament, the Regicides, our worthy friends, (I call them by advance and by courtefy what by law I fhall be obliged to call them hereafter) our worthy friends, I fay, renew and enforce the former declaration concerning our faith and fincerity, which they pinned to our paffport. On three other points which

which run through all their declarations, they are more explicit than ever.

First, they more directly undertake to be the real reprefentatives of the people of this kingdom: and on a fuppofition in which they agree with our parliamentary reformers, that the Houfe of Commons is not that Reprefentative, the function being vacant, they, as our true conftitutional organ, inform his Majefty and the world of the fenfe of the nation. They tell us that " the Englifh people fee " with regret his Majefty's Government fquandering " away the funds which had been granted to him." This aftonifhing affumption of the publick voice of England, is but a flight foretafte of the ufurpation which, on a peace, we may be affured they will make of all the powers in all the parts of our vaffal conftitution. " If it be thus in the green leaf, " what will it be in the dry?"

Next they tell us as a condition to our treaty, that " this Government muft abjure the unjuft ha- " tred it bears to them, and at laft open it's ears " to the voice of humanity."—Truely this is even from her an extraordinary demand. Hitherto it feems we have put wax into our ears to fhut them up againft the tender, foothing ftrains, in the *affettuofo* of humanity, warbled from the throats of Reubel, Carnot, Tallien, and the whole chorus of

I   Confifcators,

Confifcators, domiciliary Vifitors, Committee-men of Refearch, Jurors and Prefidents of Revolutionary Tribunals, Regicides, Affaffins, Maffacrers, and Septembrizers. It is not difficult to difcern what fort of humanity our Government is to learn from thefe fyren fingers. Our Government alfo I admit, with fome reafon, as a ftep towards the propofed fraternity, is required to abjure the unjuft hatred which it bears to this body of honour and virtue. I thank God I am neither a Minifter nor a leader of Oppofition. I proteft I cannot do what they defire, if I were under the guillotine, or as they ingenioufly and pleafantly exprefs " it, looking out of. the little national window." Even at that opening I could receive none of their light. I am fortified againft all fuch affections by the declaration of the Government, which I muft yet confider as lawful, made on the 29th of October 1793*, and ftill ringing in my ears.
This

---

* " In their place has fucceeded a fyftem deftructive of. all
" publick order, maintained by profcriptions, exiles and confif-
" cations without number : by arbitrary imprifonment; by maf-
" facres which cannot be remembered without horror ; and at
" length by the execrable murder of a juft and beneficent So-
" vereign, and of the illuftrious Princefs, who, with an un-
" fhaken firmnefs, has fhared all the misfortunes of her Royal
" Confort, his protracted fufferings, his cruel captivity and his
" ignominious death."—" They (the allies) have had to en-
" counter acts of aggreffion without pretext, open violations of
" all treaties, unprovoked declarations of war; in a word,
" whatever

This declaration was tranfmitted not only to all
our commanders by fea and land, but to our Minifters in every Court of Europe. It is the moft
eloquent and highly finifhed in the ftyle, the moft
judicious

" whatever corruption, intrigue or violence could effect for the
" purpofe fo openly avowed, of fubverting all the inftitutions
" of fociety, and of extending over all the nations of Europe
" that confufion, which has produced the mifery of France."—
    " This ftate of things cannot exift in France without in-
" volving all the furrounding powers in one common danger,
" without giving them the right, without impofing it upon them
" as a duty, to ftop the progrefs of an evil, which exifts only by
" the fucceffive violation of all law and all property, and which
" attacks the fundamental principles by which mankind is united
" in the bonds of civil fociety."—" The King would impofe
" none other-than equitable and moderate conditions, not fuch
" as the expence, the rifques and the facrifices of the war might
" juftify; but fuch as his Majefty thinks himfelf under the in-
" difpenfible neceffity of requiring, with a view to thefe confi-
" derations, and ftill more to that of his own fecurity and of
" the future tranquillity of Europe. His Majefty defires nothing
" more fincerely than thus to terminate a war, which he in vain
" endeavoured to avoid, and all the calamities of which, as now
" experienced by France, are to be attributed only to the ambi-
" tion, the perfidy and the violence of thofe, whofe crimes have
" involved their own country in mifery, and difgraced all civi-
" lized nations."—" The King promifes on his part the fufpen-
" fion of hoftilities, friendfhip, and (as far as the courfe of
" events will allow, of which the will of man cannot difpofe)
" fecurity and protection to all thofe who, by declaring for a
" monarchical form of Government, fhall fhake off the yoke of
" fanguinary anarchy; of that anarchy which has broken all
" the moft facred bonds of fociety, diffolved all the relations of
I 2   " civil

judicious in the choice of topicks, the moſt orderly in the arrangement, and the moſt rich in the colouring, without employing the ſmalleſt degree of exaggeration, of any ſtate paper that has ever yet appeared. An ancient writer, Plutarch, I think it is, quotes ſome verſes on the eloquence of Pericles, who is called " the only orator that " left ſtings in the minds of his hearers." Like his, the eloquence of the declaration, not contradicting, but enforcing ſentiments of the trueſt humanity, has left ſtings that have penetrated more than ſkin-deep into my mind ; and never can they be extracted by all the ſurgery of murder; never can the throbbings they have created, be aſſuaged by all the emollient cataplaſms of robbery and confiſcation.

The third point which they have more clearly expreſſed than ever, is of equal importance with

" civil life, violated every right, confounded every duty ; which " uſes the name of liberty to exerciſe the moſt cruel tyranny, " to annihilate all property, to ſeize on all poſſeſſions; which " founds it's power on the pretended conſent of the people, and " itſelf carries fire and ſword through extenſive provinces for " having demanded their laws, their religion and their *lawful* " *Sovereign.*"

Declaration ſent by his Majeſty's command to the Commanders of his Majeſty's fleets and armies employed againſt France, and to his Majeſty's Miniſters employed at foreign Courts.

Whitehall, Oct. 29, 1793.

the

the reft; and with them furnifhes a complete view
of the Regicide fyftem. For they demand as a
condition, without which our ambaffador of obe-
dience cannot be received with any hope of fuccefs, that he fhall be " provided with full powers
" to negociate a peace between the French Repub-
" lick and Great Britain, and to conclude it *defi-*
" *nitively* between the TWO powers." With their
fpear they draw a circle about us. They will hear
nothing of a joint treaty. We muft make a peace
feparately from our allies. We muft, as the very
firft and preliminary ftep, be guilty of that perfidy
towards our friends and affociates, with which they
reproach us in our tranfactions with them our
enemies. We are called upon fcandaloufly to
betray the fundamental fecurities to ourfelves and
to all nations. In my opinion, (it is perhaps but
a poor one) if we are meanly bold enough to fend
an ambaffador, fuch as this official note of the enemy requires, we cannot even difpatch our emiffary
without danger of being charged with a breach of
our alliance. Government now underftands the
full meaning of the paffport.

Strange revolutions have happened in the ways of
thinking and in the feelings of men: But, it requires a very extraordinary coalition of parties indeed, and a kind of unheard of unanimity
in public Councils, which can impofe this new-
difcovered

difcovered fyftem of negociation, as found national
policy on the underftanding of a fpectator of this
wonde ful fcene, who judges on the principles of
any thing he ever before faw, read, or heard of,
and above all, on the underftanding of a perfon
who has had in his eye the tranfactions of the laft
feven years.

I know it is fuppofed, that if good terms of
capitulation are not granted, after we have thus
fo repeatedly hung out the white flag, the national
fpirit will revive with tenfold ardour. This is
an experiment cautioufly to be made.. *Reculer
pour mieux fauter*, according to the French by-
word, cannot be trufted to as a general rule of conduct. To diet a man into weaknefs and langour,
afterwards to give him the greater ftrength, has
more of the empirick than the rational phyfician.
It is true that fome perfons have been kicked into
courage; and this is no bad hint to give to thofe
who are too forward and liberal in beftowing infults and outrages on their paffive companions.
But fuch a courfe does not at firft view appear a
well-chofen difcipline to form men to a nice fenfe
of honour, or a quick refentment of injuries. A
long habit of humiliation does not feem a very
good preparative to manly and vigorous fentiment. It may not leave, perhaps, enough of
energy in the mind fairly to difcern what are good

terms

terms or what are not. Men low and difpirited may regard thofe terms as not at all amifs, which in another ftate of mind they would think intoler-able : if they grew peevifh in this ftate of mind, they may be roufed, not againft the enemy whom they have been taught to fear, but againft the Miniftry*, who are more within their reach, and who have refufed conditions that are not unfeafonable, from power that they have been taught to confider as irrefiftible.

If all that for fome months I have heard have the leaft foundation, I hope it has not, the Minifters are, perhaps, not quite fo much to be blamed, as their condition is to be lamented. I have been given to underftand, that thefe pro-ceedings are not in their origin properly theirs. It is faid that there is a fecret in the Houfe of Commons. It is faid that Minifters act not accord-ing to the votes, but according to the difpofitions, of the majority. I hear that the minority has long fince fpoken the general fenfe of the nation ; and that to prevent thofe who compofe it from hav-ing the open and avowed lead in that houfe, or perhaps in both Houfes, it was neceffary to pre-occupy their ground, and to take their pro-pofitions out of their mouths, even with the ha-

* Ut lethargicus hic, cum fit pugil, et medicum urget.—Hor.

zard

ʒard of being afterwards reproached with a compliance which it was forefeen would be fruitlefs.

If the general difpofition of the people be, as I
hear it is, for an immediate peace with Regicide,
without fo much as confidering our publick and
folemn engagements to the party in France whofe
caufe we had efpoufed, or the engagements expreffed in our general alliances, not only without
an enquiry into the terms, but with a certain knowledge that none but the worft terms will be offered,
it is all over with us. It is ftrange, but it may
be true, that as the danger from Jacobinifm is
increafed in my eyes and in yours, the fear of it is
leffened in the eyes of many people who formerly
regarded it with horror. It feems, they act under the impreffion of terrors of another fort, which
have frightened them out of their firft appre-
henfions. But let their fears or their hopes, or
their defires, be what they will, they fhould recollect, that they who would make peace without a
previous knowledge of the terms, make a furrender. They are conquered. They do not treat;
they receive the law. Is this the difpofition of the
people of England? Then the people of England
are contented to feek in the kindnefs of a foreign
fyftematick enemy combined with a dangerous
faction at home, a fecurity which they cannot find

in

in their own patriotifm and their own courage. They are willing to truft to the fympathy of Regicides, the guarantee of the Britifh Monarchy. They are content to reft their religion on the piety of atheifts by eftablifhment. They are fatisfied to feek in the clemency of practifed murderers the fecurity of their lives. They are pleafed to confide their property to the fafeguard of thofe who are robbers by inclination, intereft, habit, and fyftem. If this be our deliberate mind, truly we deferve to lofe, what it is impoffible we fhould long retain, the name of a nation.

In matters of State, a conftitutional competence to act,. is in many cafes the fmalleft part of the queftion. Without difputing (God forbid I fhould difpute) the fole competence of the King and the Parliament, each in it's province, to decide on war and peace, I venture to fay, no war *can* be long carried on againft the will of the people. This war, in particular, cannot be carried on unlefs they are enthufiaftically in favour of it. Acquiefcence will not do. There muft be zeal. Univerfal zeal in fuch a caufe, and at fuch a time as this is, cannot be looked for; neither is it neceffary. A zeal in the larger part carries the force of the whole. Without this, no Government, certainly not our Government, is capable of a great war. None of the ancient regular Governments have wherewithal

K   to

to fight abroad with a foreign foe, and at home to overcome repining, reluctance, and chicane. It must be some portentous thing, like Regicide France, that can exhibit such a prodigy. Yet even she, the mother of monsters, more prolifick than the country of old called *Ferax monstrorum*, shews symptoms of being almost effete already; and she will be so, unless the fallow of a peace comes to recruit her fertility. But whatever may be represented concerning the meanness of the popular spirit, I, for one, do not think so desperately of the British nation. Our minds, as I said, are light, but they are not depraved. We are dreadfully open to delusion and to dejection; but we are capable of being animated and undeceived.

It cannot be concealed. We are a divided people. But in divisions, where a part is to be taken, we are to make a muster of our strength. I have often endeavoured to compute and to class those who, in any political view, are to be called the people. Without doing something of this sort we must proceed absurdly. We should not be much wiser, if we pretended to very great accuracy in our estimate: But I think, in the calculation I have made, the error cannot be very material. In England and Scotland, I compute that those of adult age, not declining in life, of tolerable leisure for such discussions, and of some means of information,

mation, more or lefs, and who are above menial dependence, (or what virtually is fuch) may amount to about four hundred thoufand. There is fuch a thing as a natural reprefentative of the people. This body is that reprefentative; and on this body, more than on the legal conftituent, the artificial re-prefentative depends. This is the Britifh pub-lick; and it is a publick very numerous. The reft, when feeble, are the objects of protection; when ftrong, the means of force. They who affect to confider that part of us in any other light, in-fult while they cajole us; they do not want us for counfellors in deliberation, but to lift us as fol-diers for battle.

Of thefe four hundred thoufand political citi-zens, I look upon one fifth, or about eighty thou-fand, to be pure Jacobins; utterly incapable of amendment; objects of eternal vigilance; and when they break out, of legal conftraint. On thefe, no reafon, no argument, no example, no vene-rable authority, can have the flighteft influence. They defire a change; and they will have it if they can. If they cannot have it by Englifh cabal, they will make no fort of fcruple of having it by the cabal of France, into which already they are virtually incorporated. It is only their affured and confident expectation of the advantages of French fraternity and the approaching bleffings of

Regicide

Regicide intercourse, that skins over their mischievous dispositions with a momentary quiet.

This minority is great and formidable. I do not know whether if I aimed at the total overthrow of a kingdom, I should wish to be encumbered with a larger body of partizans. They are more easily disciplined and directed than if the number were greater. These, by their spirit of intrigue, and by their restless agitating activity, are of a force far superior to their numbers; and if times grew the least critical, have the means of debauching or intimidating many of those who are now found, as well as of adding to their force large bodies of the more passive part of the nation. This minority is numerous enough to make a mighty cry for peace, or for war, or for any object they are led vehemently to desire. By passing from place to place with a velocity incredible, and diversifying their character and description, they are capable of mimicking the general voice. We must not always judge of the generality of the opinion by the noise of the acclamation.

The majority, the other four fifths, is perfectly sound; and of the best possible disposition to religion, to government, to the true and undivided interest of their country. Such men are naturally disposed to peace. They who are in possession
of

of all they wifh are languid and improvident.
With this fault, (and I admit it's exiftence in
all it's extent) they would not endure to hear
of a peace that led to the ruin of every thing for
which peace is dear to them. However, the defire
of peace is effentially the weak fide of that kind of
men. All men that are ruined, are ruined on the fide
of their natural propenfities. There they are un-
guarded. Above all, good men do not fufpect that
their deftruction is attempted through their virtues.
This their enemies are perfectly aware of: And
accordingly, they, the moft turbulent of mankind,
who never made a fcruple to fhake the tranquillity of their country to it's center, raife a continual
cry for peace with France. Peace with Regicide,
and war with the reft of the world, is their
motto. From the beginning, and even whilft the
French gave the blows, and we hardly oppofed
the *vis inertiæ* to their efforts, from that day to
this hour, like importunate Guinea-fowls crying
one note day and night, they have called for
peace.

In this they are, as I confefs in all things they
are, perfectly confiftent. They who wifh to unite
themfelves to your enemies, naturally defire, that
you fhould difarm yourfelf by a peace with thefe
enemies. But it paffes my conception, how they,
who wifh well to their country on it's antient fyf-

tem

tem of laws and manners, come not to be doubly
alarmed, when they find nothing but a clamor for
peace, in the mouths of the men on earth the leaft
difpofed to it in their natural or in their habitual
character.

I have a good opinion of the general abilities of
the Jacobins : not that I fuppofe them better born
than others ; but ftrong paffions awaken the faculties. They fuffer not a particle of the man to be loft.
The fpirit of enterprife gives to this defcription the
full ufe of all their native energies. If I have
reafon to conceive that my enemy, who, as fuch,
muft have an intereft in my deftruction, is alfo a
perfon of difcernment and fagacity, then I muft
be quite fure, that in a conteft, the object he violently purfues, is the very thing by which my ruin
is likely to be the moft perfectly accomplifhed.
Why do the Jacobins cry for peace ? Becaufe they
know, that this point gained, the reft will follow
of courfe. On our part, why are all the rules of
prudence, as fure as the laws of material nature, to
be at this time reverfed ? How comes it, that now
for the firft time, men think it right to be governed
by the counfels of their enemies ? Ought they not
rather to tremble, when they are perfuaded to tra-
vel on the fame road ; and to tend to the fame
place of reft ?

The

The minority I fpeak of, is not fufceptible of an impreffion from the topics of argument, to be ufed to the larger part of the community. I therefore do not addrefs to them any part of what I have to fay. The more forcibly I drive my arguments againft their fyftem, fo as to make an impreffion where I wifh to make it, the more ftrongly I rivet them in their fentiments. As for us, who compofe the far larger, and what I call the far better part of the people ; let me fay, that we have not been quite fairly dealt with when called to this deli-beration. The Jacobin minority have been abun-dantly fupplied with ftores and provifions of all kinds towards their warfare. No fort of argumen-tative materials, fuited to their purpofes, have been withheld. Falfe they are, unfound, fophiftical ; but they are regular in their direction. They all bear one way ; and they all go to the fupport of the fubftantial merits of their caufe. The others have not had the queftion fo much as fairly ftated to them.

There has not been in this century, any foreign peace or war, in it's origin, the fruit of popular defire ; except the war that was made with Spain in 1739. Sir Robert Walpole was forced into the war by the people, who were inflamed to this meafure by the moft leading politicians, by the firft orators, and the greateft poets of

the

the time. For that war, Pope fung his dying
notes. For that war, Johnfon, in more energetic
ftrains, employed the voice of his early genius.
For that war, Glover diftinguifhed himfelf in the
way in which his mufe was the moft natural and
happy. The crowd readily followed the politicians in the cry for a war, which threatened little
bloodfhed, and which promifed victories that were
attended with fomething more folid than glory. A
war with Spain was a war of plunder. In the
prefent conflict with Regicide, Mr. Pitt has
not hitherto had, nor will perhaps for a few
days have, many prizes to hold out in the
lottery of war, to tempt the lower part of our
character. He can only maintain it by an ap-
peal to the higher; and to thofe, in whom that
higher part is the moft predominant, he muft look
the moft for his fupport. Whilft he holds out no
inducements to the wife, nor bribes to the avaricious, he may be forced by a vulgar cry into a
peace ten times more ruinous than the moft dif-
aftrous war. The weaker he is in the fund of motives which apply to our avarice, to our lazinefs,
and to our laffitude, if he means to carry the war to
any end at all, the ftronger he ought to be in his
addreffes to our magnanimity and to our reafon.

In ftating that Walpole was driven by a popular
clamour into a meafure not to be juftified, I do
not

not mean wholly to excufe his conduct. My time
of obfervation did not exactly coincide with that
event; but I read much of the controverfies then
carried on. Several years after the contefts of parties had ceafed, the people were amufed, and in a
degree warmed with them. The events of that
æra feemed then of magnitude, which the revolutions of our time have reduced to parochial importance; and the debates, which then fhook the
nation, now appear of no higher moment than a
difcuffion in a veftry. When I was very young,
a general fafhion told me I was to admire fome of
the writings againft that Minifter; a little more
maturity taught me as much to defpife them. I
obferved one fault in his general proceeding. He
never manfully put forward the entire ftrength of
his caufe. He temporifed; he managed; and
adopting very nearly the fentiments of his adverfaries, he oppofed their inferences. This, for a political commander, is the choice of a weak poft.
His adverfaries had the better of the argument, as
he handled it, not as the reafon and juftice of his
caufe enabled him to manage it. I fay this, after
having feen, and with fome care examined, the original documents concerning certain important
tranfactions of thofe times. They perfectly fatisfied me of the extreme injuftice of that war, and
of the falfehood of the colours, which to his own
ruin, and guided by a miftaken policy, he fuf-

L   fered

fered to be daubed over that meafure. Some years after, it was my fortune to converfe with many of the principal actors againft that Minifter, and with thofe; who principally excited that clamour. None of them, no not one, did in the leaft defend the meafure, or attempt to juftify their conduct. They condemned it as freely as they would have done in commenting upon any proceeding in hif-tory, in which they were totally unconcerned. Thus it will be. They who ftir up the people to improper defires, whether of peace or war, will be condemned by themfelves. They who weakly yield to them will be condemned by hiftory.

In my opinion, the prefent Miniftry are as far from doing full juftice to their caufe in this war, as Walpole was from doing juftice to the peace which at that time he was willing to preferve. They throw the light on one fide only of their cafe ; though it is impoffible they fhould not obferve, that the other fide which is kept in the fhade, has it's importance too. They muft know, that France is formidable, not only as fhe is France, but as fhe is Jacobin France. They knew from the beginning that the Jacobin party was not confined to that country. They knew, they felt, the ftrong difpofition of the fame faction in both countries to communicate and to co-operate. For fome time paft, thefe two points

have

have been kept, and even induftrioufly kept, out of
fight. France is confidered as merely a foreign
Power; and the feditious Englifh only as a domeftick faction. The merits of the war with the former have been argued folely on political grounds.
To prevent the mifchievous doctrines of the latter,
from corrupting our minds, matter and argument
have been fupplied abundantly, and even to fur-
feit, on the excellency of our own government.
But nothing has been done to make us feel in
what manner the fafety of that Government is
connected with the principle and with the iffue of
this war. For any thing, which in the late difcuffion has appeared, the war is entirely collateral
to the ftate of Jacobinifm; as truly a foreign war
to us and to all our home concerns, as the war
with Spain in 1739, about *Garda-Coftas*, the
Madrid Convention, and the fable of Captain
Jenkins's ears,

Whenever the adverfe party has raifed a cry for
peace with the Regicide, the anfwer has been little
more than this, " that the Adminiftration wifhed ior
" fuch a peace, full as much as the Oppofition ; but
" that the time was not convenient for making it."
Whatever elfe has been faid was much in the fame
fpirit. Reafons of this kind never touched the fubftantial merits of the war. They were in the nature of dilatory pleas, exceptions of form, pre-

vious

vious queſtions. Accordingly all the arguments againſt a compliance with what was repreſented as the popular deſire, (urged on with all poſſible vehemence and earneſtneſs by the Jacobins) have appeared flat and languid, feeble and evaſive. They appeared to aim only at gaining time. They never entered into the peculiar and diſtinctive character of the war. They ſpoke neither to the underſtanding nor to the heart. Cold as ice themſelves, they never could kindle in our breaſts a ſpark of that zeal, which is neceſſary to a conflict with an adverſe zeal; much leſs were they made to infuſe into our minds, that ſtubborn perſevering ſpirit, which alone is capable of bearing up againſt thoſe viciſſitudes of fortune, which will probably occur, and thoſe burthens which muſt be inevitably borne in a long war. I ſpeak it emphatically, and with a deſire that it ſhould be marked, in a *long* war; becauſe, without ſuch a war, no experience has yet told us, that a dangerous power has ever been reduced to meaſure or to reaſon. I do not throw back my view to the Peloponneſian war of twenty-ſeven years; nor to two of the Punick wars, the firſt of twenty-four, the ſecond of eighteen; nor to the more recent war concluded by the treaty of Weſtphalia, which continued, I think, for thirty. I go to what is but juſt fallen behind living memory, and immediately touches our own country. Let the portion of our hiſtory

from

from the year 1689 to 1713 be brought before us. We fhall find, that in all that period of twenty-four years, there were hardly five that could be called a feafon of peace; and the interval between the two wars was in reality, nothing more than a very active preparation for renovated hoftility. During that period, every one of the propofitions of peace came from the enemy: The firft, when they were accepted, at the peace of Ryfwick; The fecond, where they were rejected at the congrefs at Gertruydenburgh; The laft, when the war ended by the treaty of Utrecht. Even then, a very great part of the nation, and that which contained by far the moft intelligent ftatefmen, was againft the conclufion of the war. I do not enter into the merits of that queftion as between the parties. I only ftate the exiftence of that opinion as a fact, from whence you may draw fuch an inference as you think properly arifes from it.

It is for us at prefent to recollect what we have been; and to confider what, if we pleafe, we may be ftill. At the period of thofe wars, our principal ftrength was found in the refolution of the people; that in the refolution of a part only and of the then whole, which bore no proportion to our exifting magnitude. England and Scotland were not united at the beginning of that mighty ftruggle. When, in the courfe of the conteft,

they

they were conjoined, it was in a raw, an ill-ce-
mented, an unproductive union. For the whole
duration of he war, and long after, the names, and
other outward and vifible figns of approximation,
rather augmented than diminifhed our infular
feuds. They were rather the caufes of new difcontents and new troubles, than promoters of cordia-
lity and affection. The now fingle and potent
Great Britain was then not only two countries,
but, from the party heats in both, and the divi-
fions formed in each of them, each of the old kingdoms within itfelf in effect was made up of two
hoftile nations. Ireland, now fo large a fource
of the common opulence and power, which wifely
managed might be made much more beneficial
and much more effective, was then the heavieft of
the burthens. An army not much lefs than forty
thoufand men, was drawn from the general effort,
to keep that kingdom in a poor, unfruitful, and re-
fourcelefs fubjection.

Such was the ftate of the empire. The ftate
of our finances was worfe, if poffible. Every
branch of the revenue became lefs productive after
the Revolution. Silver, not as now a fort of counter, but the body of the current coin, was reduced
fo low, as not to have above three parts in four of
the value in the fhilling. It required a dead expence of three millions fterling to renew the coin-
age.

age. Publick credit, that great but ambiguous principle, which has fo often been predicted as the caufe of our certain ruin, but which for a century has been the conftant companion, and often the means, of our profperity and greatnefs, had it's origin, and was cradled, I may fay, in bankruptcy and beggary. At this day we have feen parties contending to be admitted, at a moderate premium, to advance eighteen millions to the Exchequer. For infinitely fmaller loans, the Chancellor of the Exchequer of that day, Montagu, the father of publick credit, counter-fecuring the State by the appearance of the city, with the Lord-Mayor of London at his fide, was obliged, like an agent at an election, to go cap in hand from fhop to fhop, to borrow an hundred pound and even fmaller fums. When made up in driblets as they could, their beft fecurities were at an intereft of 12 per cent. Even the paper of the Bank (now at par with cafh, and even fometimes preferred to it) was often at a difcount of twenty per cent. By this the ftate of the reft may be judged.

As to our commerce, the imports and exports of the nation, now fix and forty million, did not then amount to ten. The inland trade, which is commonly paffed by in this fort of eftimates, but which, in part growing out of the foreign, and connected with it, is more advantageous, and more fubftan-

tially

tially nutritive to the State, is not only grown in a proportion of near five to one as the foreign, but has been augmented, at leaſt, in a tenfold proportion. When I came to England, I remember but one river navigation, the rate of carriage on which was limited by an Act of Parliament. It was made in the reign of William the Third ; I mean that of the Aire and Calder. The rate was ſettled at thirteen pence. So high a price demonſtrated the feeblenefs of thefe beginnings of our inland intercouſe. In my time, one of the longeſt and ſharpeſt conteſts I remember in your Houſe, and which rather refembled a violent contention amongſt national parties than a local difpute, was, as well as I can recollect, to hold the price up to threepence. Even this, which a very fcanty juſtice to the proprietors required, was done with infinite difficulty. As to private credit, there were not, as I beſt remember, twelve Bankers ſhops at that time out of London. In this their number, when I firſt faw the country, I cannot be quite exact; but certainly thoſe machines of domeſtick credit were then very few indeed. They are now in almoſt every market town : and this circumſtance (whether the thing be carried to an exceſs or not) demonſtrates the aſtoniſhing encreaſe of private confidence, of general circulation, and of internal commerce ; an encreaſe out of all proportion to the growth of the foreign trade.

Our

Our naval ſtrength in the time of King William's war was nearly matched by that of France; and though conjoined with Holland, then a maritime Power hardly inferior to our own, even with that force we were not always victorious. Though finally ſuperior, the allied fleets experienced many unpleaſant reverſes on their own element. In two years three thouſand veſſels were taken from the Engliſh trade. On the continent we loſt almoſt every battle we fought.

In 1697, it is not quite an hundred years ago, in that ſtate of things, amidſt the general debaſement of the coin, the fall of the ordinary revenue, the failure of all the extraordinary ſupplies, the ruin of commerce and the almoſt total extinction of an infant credit, the Chancellor of the Exchequer himſelf whom we have juſt ſeen begging from door to door—came forward to move a reſolution, full of vigour, in which far from being diſcouraged by the generally adverſe fortune, and the long continuance of the war, the Commons agreed to addreſs the Crown in the following manly, ſpirited, and truly animating ſtyle.

" This is the EIGHTH year in which your Ma-
" jeſty's moſt dutiful and loyal ſubjects the Com-
" mons in Parliament aſſembled, have aſſiſted your
" Majeſty with large ſupplies for carrying on a juſt

M   " and

" and neceffary war, in defence of our religion, and
" prefervation of our laws, and vindication of the
" rights and liberties of the people of England.

Afterwards they proceed in this manner :—
" To fhew to your Majefty and all Chriftendom,
" that the Commons of England will not be
" *amufed* or diverted from their firm refolutions of
" obtaining by WAR, a fafe and honourable peace,
" we do in the name of thofe we reprefent, renew
" our affurances to fupport your Majefty and your
" Government againft all your enemies at home
" and abroad; and that we will effectually affift
" you in carrying on the war againft France."

The amufement and diverfion they fpeak of,
was the fuggeftion of a treaty *propofed by the
enemy*, and announced from the Throne. Thus
the people of England felt in the *eighth*, not in the
fourth year of the war. No fighing or panting after negociation; no motions from the Oppofition
to force the Miniftry into a peace ; no meffages
from Minifters to palfy and deaden the refolution
of Parliament or the fpirit of the nation. They
did not fo much as advife the King to liften to the
propofitions of the enemy, nor to feek for peace
but through the mediation of a vigorous war. This
addrefs was moved in an hot, a divided, a factious,
and in a great part, difaffected Houfe of Commons,
and it was carried *nemine contradicente*.

While

While that firſt war (which was ill ſmothered by the treaty of Ryſwick) ſlept in the thin aſhes of a ſeeming peace, a new conflagration was in it's immediate cauſes. A freſh and a far greater war was in preparation. A year had hardly elapſed when arrangements were made for renewing the conteſt with tenfold fury. The ſteps which were taken, at that time, to compoſe, to reconcile, to unite, and to diſcipline all Europe againſt the growth of France, certainly furniſh to a ſtateſman the fineſt and moſt intereſting part in the hiſtory of that great period. It formed the maſter-piece of King William's policy, dexterity, and perſeverance. Full of the idea of preſerving, not only a local civil liberty united with order, to our country, but to embody it in the political liberty, the order, and the independence of nations united under a natural head, the King called upon his Parliament to put itſelf into a poſture " *to preſerve to England the* " *weight and influence it at preſent had on the coun-* " *cils and affairs* ABROAD. It will be requiſite *Eu-* " *rope* ſhould ſee you will not be wanting to your- " ſelves."

Baffled as that Monarch was, and almoſt heart-broken at the diſappointment he met with in the mode he firſt propoſed for that great end, he held on his courſe. He was faithful to his object; and in councils, as in arms, over and over again

M 2   repulſed,

repulſed, over and over again he returned to the
charge. All the mortifications he had ſuffered
from the laſt Parliament, and the greater he had to
apprehend from that newly choſen, were not capable of relaxing the vigour of his mind. He was
in Holland when he combined the vaſt plan of his
foreign negociations. When he came to open
his deſign to his Miniſters in England, even the
ſober firmneſs of Somers, the undaunted reſolution of Shrewſbury, and the adventurous ſpirit
of Montagu and Orford, were ſtaggered. They
were not yet mounted to the elevation of the
King. The Cabinet met on the ſubject at Tun-
bridge Wells the 28th of Auguſt, 1698; and
there, Lord Somers holding the pen, after expreſ-
ſing doubts on the ſtate of the continent, which
they ultimately refer to the King, as beſt informed, they give him a moſt diſcouraging portrait of
the ſpirit of this nation. " So far as relates to
" England," ſay theſe Miniſters, " it would be
" want of duty not to give your Majeſty this clear
" account, that *there* is a *deadneſs and want of ſpi-*
" *rit in the nation univerſally*, ſo as not to be at
" all diſpoſed to *entering into a new war.* That
" they ſeem to be *tired out with taxes* to a degree
" beyond what was diſcerned, till it appeared upon
" occaſion of the *late elections.* This is the truth
" of the fact upon which your Majeſty will deter-
" mine what reſolution ought to be taken."

His

His Majefty did determine; and did take and purfue his refolution. In all the tottering imbecility of a new Government, and with Parliament totally unmanageable, he perfevered. He perfevered to expel the fears of his people, by his fortitude—To fteady their ficklenefs, by his conftancy—To expand their narrow prudence, by his enlarged wifdom—To fink their factious temper in his public fpirit.—In fpite of his people he refolved to make them great and glorious; to make England, inclined to fhrink into her narrow felf, the Arbitrefs of Europe, the tutelary Angel of the human race. In fpite of the Minifters, who ftaggered under the weight that his mind impofed upon theirs, unfupported as they felt themfelves by the popular fpirit, he infufed into them his own foul; he renewed in them their ancient heart; he rallied them in the fame caufe.

It required fome time to accomplifh this work. The people were firft gained, and through them their diftracted reprefentatives. Under the influence of King William Holland had refifted the allurements of every feduction, and had refifted the terrors of every menace. With Hannibal at her gates, fhe had nobly and magnanimoufly refufed all feparate treaty, or any thing which might for a moment appear to divide her affection or her intereft, or even to diftinguifh her in identity from England.
Having

Having settled the great point of the consolida-
tion (which he hoped would be eternal) of the
countries made for a common interest, and common sentiment, the King, in his message to both
Houses, calls their attention to the affairs of
the *States General.* The House of Lords was
perfectly found, and entirely impressed with the
wisdom and dignity of the King's proceedings.
In answer to the message, which you will observe
was narrowed to a single point, (the danger of
the States General) after the usual professions of
zeal for his service, the Lords opened themselves
at large. They go far beyond the demands of
the message. They express themselves as follows:
" We take this occasion *further* to assure your
" Majesty, that we are sensible of the *great and*
" *imminent danger to which the States General are*
" *exposed. And we perfectly agree with them in be-*
" *lieving that their safety and ours are so inseparably*
" *united, that whatsoever is ruin to the one must be*
" *fatal to the other.*

" We humbly desire your Majesty will be pleas-
" ed, *not only* to make good all the articles of any
" *former* treaties to the Sates General, but that you
" will enter into a strict league, offensive and de-
" fensive, with them, *for their common preservation:*
" *and that you will invite into it all Princes and*
" *States*

" *States who are concerned in the prefent vifible dan-*
" *ger, arifing from the union of France and Spain.*

" And we further defire your Majefty, that you
" will be pleafed to enter into fuch alliances with
" the *Emperor*, as your Majefty fhall think fit,
" purfuant to the ends of the treaty of 1689; to-
" wards all which we affure your Majefty of our
" hearty and fincere affiftance; not doubting, but
" whenever your Majefty fhall be obliged to be
" engaged for the defence of your allies, *and fe-*
" *curing the liberty and quiet of Europe*, Almighty
" God will protect your facred perfon in fo righte-
" ous a caufe. And that the unanimity, wealth,
" and courage of your fubjects will carry your Ma-
" jefty with honour and fuccefs *through all the*
" *difficulties of a* JUST WAR."

The Houfe of Commons was more referved; the
late popular difpofition was ftill in a great degree
prevalent in the reprefentative, after it had been
made to change in the conftituent body. The
principle of the Grand Alliance was not directly
recognized in the refolution of the Commons, nor
the war announced, though they were well aware
the alliance was formed for the war. However,
compelled by the returning fenfe of the people,
they went fo far as to fix the three great immove-
able pillars of the fafety and greatnefs of England.

as they were then, as they are now, and as they
muft ever be to the end of time. They afferted in
general terms the neceffity of fupporting Holland;
of keeping united with our allies; and maintain-
ing the liberty of Europe; though they reftricted
their vote to the fuccours ftipulated by actual
treaty. But now they were fairly embarked; they
were obliged to go with the courfe of the veffel;
and the whole nation, fplit before into an hundred
adverfe factions, with a King at it's head evidently
declining to his tomb, the whole nation, Lords,
Commons, and People, proceeded as one body,
informed by one foul. Under the Britifh union,
the union of Europe was confolidated; and it long
held together with a degree of cohefion, firmnefs,
and fidelity not known before or fince in any political combination of that extent.

Juft as the laft hand was given to this immenfe
and complicated machine, the mafter workman
died: But the work was formed on true mechanical principles; and it was as truly wrought. It
went by the impulfe it had received from the firft
mover. The man was dead: But the grand
alliance furvived, in which King William lived
and reigned. That heartlefs and difpirited people,
whom Lord Somers had reprefented, about two
years before, as dead in energy and operation,
continued that war to which it was fuppofed they
were

were unequal in mind, and in means, for near thirteen years.

For what have I entered into all this detail? To what purpofe have I recalled your view to the end of the laft century? It has been done to fhew that the Britifh Nation was then a great people— to point out how and by what means they came to be exalted above the vulgar level, and to take that lead which they affumed among mankind. To qualify us for that pre-eminence, we had then an high mind, and a conftancy unconquerable; we were then infpired with no flafhy paffions; but fuch as were durable as well as warm; fuch as cor-refponded to the great interefts we had at ftake. This force of character was infpired, as all fuch fpirit muft ever be, from above. Government gave the impulfe. As well may we fancy, that, of itfelf the fea will fwell, and that without winds the billows will infult the adverfe fhore, as that the grofs mafs of the people will be moved, and elevated, and continue by a fteady and permanent direction to bear upon one point, without the influence of fuperior authority, or fuperior mind.

This impulfe ought, in my opinion, to have been given in this war; and it ought to have been con-tinued to it at every inftant. It is made, if ever war was made, to touch all the great fprings of

N   action

action in the human breaft. It ought not to have been a war of apology. The Minifter had, in this conflict, wherewithal to glory in fuccefs; to be confoled in adverfity; to hold high his principle in all fortunes. If it were not given him to fupport the falling edifice, he ought to bury himfelf under the ruins of the civilized world. All the art of Greece, and all the pride and power of eaftern Monarchs, never heaped upon their afhes fo grand a monument.

There were days when his great mind was up to the crifis of the world he is called to act in*. His manly eloquence was equal to the elevated wifdom of fuch fentiments. But the little have triumphed over the great; an unnatural, (as it fhould feem) not an unufual victory. I am fure you cannot forget with how much uneafinefs we heard in converfation, the language of more than one gentleman at the opening of this conteft, " that he was willing to " try the war for a year or two, and if it did not " fuccced, then to vote for peace." As if war was a matter of experiment! As if you could take it up or lay it down as an idle frolick! As if the dire goddefs that prefides over it, with her murderous fpear in her hand, and her gorgon at her breaft, was a coquette to be flirted with! We ought with reverence to approach that tremendous

* See the Declaration.

divinity,

divinity, that loves courage, but commands counfel. War never leaves, where it found a nation.
It is never to be entered into without a mature
deliberation; not a deliberation lengthened out
into a perplexing indecifion, but a deliberation
leading to a fure and fixed judgment. When fo
taken up it is not to be abandoned without reafon
as valid, as fully, and as extenfively confidered.
Peace may be made as unadvifedly as war. Nothing is fo rafh as fear; and the counfels of pufil-
lanimity very rarely put off, whilft they are always
fure to aggravate, the evils from which they would
fly.

In that great war carried on againft Louis the
XIVth, for near eighteen years, Government fpared
no pains to fatisfy the nation, that though they
were to be animated by a defire of glory, glory
was not their ultimate object: but that every thing
dear to them, in religion, in law, in liberty, every
thing which as freemen, as Englifhmen, and as citizens of the great commonwealth of Chriftendom,
they had at heart, was then at ftake. This was to
know the true art of gaining the affections and
confidence of an high-minded people; this was
to underftand human nature. A danger to avert
a danger---a prefent inconvenience and fuffering to prevent a forefeen future, and a worfe
calamity---thefe are the motives that belong to

an

an animal, who, in his conſtitution, is at once adventurous and provident; circumſpect and daring;
whom his Creator has made, as the Poet ſays, " of
" large diſcourſe, looking before and after." But
never can a vehement and ſuſtained ſpirit of fortitude be kindled in a people by a war of calculation.
It has nothing that can keep the mind erect under
the guſts of adverſity. Even where men are willing, as ſometimes they are, to barter their blood for
lucre, to hazard their ſafety for the gratification of
their avarice, the paſſion, which animates them to
that ſort of conflict, like all the ſhort-ſighted paſſions, muſt ſee it's objects diſtinct and near at hand.
The paſſions of the lower order are hungry and impatient. Speculative plunder; contingent ſpoil; future, long adjourned, uncertain booty; pillage which
muſt enrich a late poſterity, and which poſſibly may
not reach to poſterity at all; theſe, for any length of
time, will never ſupport a mercenary war. The
people are in the right. The calculation of profit
in all ſuch wars is falſe. On balancing the account of ſuch wars, ten thouſand hogſheads of
ſugar are purchaſed at ten thouſand times their
price. The blood of man ſhould never be ſhed but
to redeem the blood of man. It is well ſhed for
our family, for our friends, for our God, for our
country, for our kind. The reſt is vanity; the
reſt is crime,

In

In the war of the Grand Alliance, moſt of theſe conſiderations voluntarily and naturally had their part. Some were preſſed into the ſervice. The political intereſt eaſily went in the track of the natural ſentiment. In the reverſe courſe the carriage does not follow freely. I am ſure the natural feeling, as I have juſt ſaid, is a far more predominant ingredient in this war, than in that of any other that ever was waged by this kingdom.

If the war made to prevent the union of two crowns upon one head was a juſt war, this, which is made to prevent the tearing all crowns from all heads which ought to wear them, and with the crowns to ſmite off the ſacred heads themſelves, this is a juſt war.

If a war to prevent Louis the XIVth from impoſing his religion was juſt, a war to prevent the murderers of Louis the XVIth from impoſing their irreligion upon us is juſt; a war to prevent the operation of a ſyſtem, which makes life without dignity, and death without hope, is a juſt war.

If to preſerve political independence and civil freedom to nations, was a juſt ground of war; a war to preſerve national independence, property, liberty, life, and honour, from certain univerſal havock, is a war juſt, neceſſary, manly, pious;
and

and we are bound to perfevere in it by every principle, divine and human, as long as the fyftem which menaces them all, and all equally, has an exiftence in the world.

You, who have looked at this matter with as fair and impartial an eye as can be united with a feeling heart, you will not think it an hardy affertion, when I affirm, that it were far better to be conquered by any other nation, than to have this faction for a neighbour. Before I felt myfelf authorifed to fay this, I confidered the ftate of all the countries in Europe for thefe laft three hundred years, which have been obliged to fubmit to a foreign law. In moft of thofe I found the condition of the annexed countries even better, certainly not worfe, than the lot of thofe which were the patrimony of the conquerour. They wanted fome bleffings—but they were free from many very great evils. They were rich and tranquil. Such was Artois, Flanders, Lorrain, Alfatia, under the old Government of France. Such was Silefia under the King of Pruffia. They who are to live in the vicinity of this new fabrick, are to prepare to live in perpetual confpiracies and feditions; and to end at laft, in being conquered, if not to her dominion, to her refemblance. But when we talk of conqueft by other nations, it is only to put a cafe. This is the only power in Europe by which

it

it is *poffible* we fhould be conquered. To live under the continual dread of fuch immeafurable evils is itfelf a grievous calamity. To live without the dread of them is to turn the danger into the difafter. The influence of fuch a France is equal to a war; it's example, more wafting than an hof-tile irruption. The hoftility with any other power is feparable and accidental; this power, by the very condition of it's exiftence, by it's very effential conftitution, is in a ftate of hoftility with us, and with all civilized people.*

A Government of the nature of that fet up at our very door has never been hitherto feen, or even imagined, in Europe. What our relation to it will be cannot be judged by other relations. It is a ferious thing to have a connexion with a people, who live only under pofitive, arbitrary, and change-able inftitutions; and thofe not perfected nor fup-plied, nor explained, by any common acknowledged rule of moral fcience. I remember that in one of my laft converfations with the late Lord Camden, we were ftruck much in the fame manner with the abolition in France of the law, as a fcience of methodized and artificial equity. France, fince her Revolution, is under the fway of a fect, whofe leaders have deliberately, at one ftroke, de-molifhed the whole body of that jurifprudence which France had pretty nearly in common with

* See declaration, Whitehall, October 29, 1793.

other

other civilized countries. In that jurifprudence
were contained the elements and principles of the
law of nations, the great ligament of mankind.
With the law they have of courfe deftroyed all
feminaries in which jurifprudence was taught, as
well as all the corporations eftablifhed for it's confervation. I have not heard of any country, whether in Europe or Afia, or even in Africa on this
fide of Mount Atlas, which is wholly without fome
fuch colleges and fuch corporations, except France.
No man, in a publick or private concern, can divine by what rule or principle her judgments are to
be directed; nor is there to be found a profeffor
in any Univerfity, or a practitioner in any Court,
who will hazard an opinion of what is or is not
law in France, in any cafe whatever. They have
not only annulled all their old treaties; but they
have renounced the law of nations from whence
treaties have their force. With a fixed defign
they have outlawed themfelves, and to their power
outlawed all other nations.

Inftead of the religion and the law by which
they were in a great politick communion with
the Chriftian world they have conftructed their
Republick on three bafes, all fundamentally oppofite to thofe on which the communities of Europe
are built. It's foundation is laid in Regicide; in
Jacobinifm; and in Atheifm; and it has joined to
thofe

thofe principles, a body of fyftematick manners which fecures their operation.

If I am afked how I would be underftood in the ufe of thefe terms, Regicide, Jacobinifm, Atheifm, and a fyftem of correfpondent manners and their eftablifhment, I will tell you.

I call a commonwealth *Regicide*, which lays it down as a fixed law of nature, and a fundamental right of man, that all government, not being a democracy, is an ufurpation *. That all Kings, as fuch, are ufurpers; and for being Kings, may and ought to be put to death, with their wives, families, and adherents. The commonwealth which acts uniformly upon thofe principles; and which after abolifhing every feftival of religion, choofes the moft flagrant act of a murderous Regicide treafon for a feaft of eternal commemoration, and which forces all her people to obferve it---This I call *Regicide by eftablifhment*.

---

* Nothing could be more folemn than their promulgation of this principle as a preamble to the deftructive code of their famous articles for the decompofition of fociety into whatever country they fhould enter. " La Convention Nationale, après avoir entendu le rapport de fes Comittés de Finances, de la guerre, & diplomatiques réunis, fidelle *au principe de fouveraineté de peuples qui ne lui permet pas de reconnoitre aucune inftitution qui y porte atteinte*," &c. &c. Decret fur le Rapport de Cambon. Dec. 18, 1792, and fee the fubfequent proclamation.

Jacobinifm

Jacobinifm is the revolt of the enterprifing talents of a country againft it's property. When
private men form themfelves into affociations for
the purpofe of deftroying the pre-exifting laws and
inftitutions of their country; when they fecure to
themfelves an army by dividing amongft the people
of no property, the eftates of the ancient and lawful proprietors; when a ftate recognizes thofe acts;
when it does not make confifcations for crimes,.
but makes crimes for confifcations; when it has
it's principal ftrength, and all it's refources in fuch
a violation of property; when it ftands chiefly
upon fuch a violation; maffacring by judgments,
or otherwife, thofe who make any ftruggle for
their old legal government, and their legal, heredi-
tary, or acquired poffeffions—I call this *Jacobinifm
by Eftablifhment.*

I call it *Atheifm by Eftablifhment*, when any State,
as fuch, fhall not acknowledge the exiftence of
God as a moral Governor of the World; when it
fhall offer to Him no religious or moral worfhip;
—when it fhall abolifh the Chriftian religion by a
regular decree;—when it fhall perfecute with a
cold, unrelenting, fteady cruelty, by every mode of
confifcation, imprifonment, exile, and death, all it's
minifters;—when it fhall generally fhut up, or pull
down, churches; when the few buildings which remain of this kind fhall be opened only for the purpofe
of

of making a profane apotheofis of monfters, whofe
vices and crimes have no parallel amongft men, and
whom all other men confider as objects of general
deteftation, and the ſevereſt animadverſion of law.
When, in the place of that religion of ſocial benevolence, and of individual ſelf-denial, in mockery
of all religion, they inſtitute impious, blaſphemous,
indecent theatric rites, in honour of their vitiated, perverted reaſon, and erect altars to the per-
ſonification of their own corrupted and bloody Republick;—when ſchools and ſeminaries are founded at publick expence to poiſon mankind, from generation to generation, with the horrible maxims of
this impiety;—when wearied out with inceſſant
martyrdom, and the cries of a people hungering
and thirfting for religion, they permit it, only as
a tolerated evil—I call this *Atheiſm by Eſtabliſhment.*

When to theſe eftablifhments of Regicide, of
Jacobiniſin, and of Atheiſm, you add the *corre-
ſpondent ſyſtem of manners,* no doubt can be left
on the mind of a thinking man, concerning their
determined hoftility to the human race. Manners
are of more importance than laws. Upon them, in
a great meafure the laws depend. The law touches
us but here and there, and now and then. Manners
are what vex or footh, corrupt or purify, exalt or de-
baſe, barbarize or refine us, by a conftant, fteady,

uniform,

uniform, infenfible operation, like that of the air we breathe in. They give their whole form and colour to our lives. According to their quality, they aid morals, they fupply them, or they totally deftroy them. Of this the new French Legiflators were aware; therefore, with the fame method, and under the fame authority, they fettled a fyftem of manners, the moft licentious, proftitute, and abandoned that ever has been known, and at the fame time the moft coarfe, rude; favage, and fe-rocious. Nothing in the Revolution, no, not to a phrafe or a gefture, not to the fafhion of a hat or a fhoe, was left to accident. All has been the refult of defign; all has been matter of infti-tution. No mechanical means could be devifed in favour of this incredible fyftem of wickednefs and vice, that has not been employed. The nobleft paffions, the love of glory, the love of country, have been debauched into means of it's prefervation and it's propagation. All forts of fhews and exhibitions calculated to inflame and vitiate the imagination, and pervert the moral fenfe, have been con-trived. They have fometimes brought forth five or fix hundred drunken women, calling at the bar of the Affembly for the blood of their own children, as being royalifts or conftitutionalifts. Sometimes they have got a body of wretches, calling themfelves fathers, to demand the murder of their fons; boafting that Rome had but one Brutus, but that they could fhew five hundred.

There

There were inftances, in which they inverted, and retaliated the impiety, and produced fons, who called for the execution of their parents. The foundation of their Republick is laid in moral paradoxes. Their patriotifm is always prodigy. All thofe inftances to be found in hiftory, whether real or fabulous, of a doubtful publick fpirit, at which morality is perplexed, reafon is ftaggered, and from which affrighted nature recoils, are their chofen, and almoft fole examples for the inftruction of their youth.

The whole drift of their inftitution is contrary to that of the wife Legiflators of all countries, who aimed at improving inftincts into morals, and at grafting the virtues on the ftock of the natural affections. They, on the contrary, have omitted no pains to eradicate every benevolent and noble propenfity in the mind of men. In their culture it is a rule always to graft virtues on vices. They think every thing unworthy of the name of publick virtue, unlefs it indicates violence on the private. All their new inftitutions, (and with them every thing is new) ftrike at the root of our focial nature. Other Legiflators, knowing that marriage is the origin of all relations, and confequently the firft element of all duties, have endeavoured, by every art, to make it facred. The Chriftian Religion, by confining it to the pairs, and by rendering that relation indiffo-

luble

luble, has, by thefe two things, done more towards
the peace, happinefs, fettlement, and civilization
of the world, than by any other part in this whole
fcheme of Divine Wifdom. The direct contrary
courfe has been taken in the Synagogue of Anti-
chrift, I mean in that forge and manufactory of all
evil, the fect which predominated in the Conftituent Affembly of 1789. Thofe monfters employed the fame, or greater induftry, to defecrate
and degrade that State, which other Legiflators
have ufed to render it holy and honourable. By a
ftrange, uncalled for declaration, they pronounced,
that marriage was no better than a common, civil
contract. It was one of their ordinary tricks, to
put their fentiments into the mouths of certain
perfonated characters, which they theatrically ex-
hibited at the bar of what ought to be a ferious
Affembly. One of thefe was brought out in the
figure of a proftitute, whom they called by the
affected name of " a mother without being a
wife." This creature they made to call for a
repeal of the incapacities, which in civilized States
are put upon baftards. The proftitutes of the Affembly gave to this their puppet the fanction of
their greater impudence. In confequence of the
principles laid down, and the manners authorifed,
baftards were not long after put on the footing of the
iffue of lawful unions. Proceeding in the fpirit of
the firft authors of their conftitution, fucceeding af-
                                          femblies

femblies went the full length of the principle, and gave a licence to divorce at the mere pleafure of either party, and at a month's notice. With them the matrimonial connexion is brought into fo degraded a ftate of concubinage, that, I believe, none of the wretches in London, who keep warehoufes of infamy, would give out one of their victims to private cuftody on fo fhort and infolent a tenure. There was indeed a kind of profligate equity in thus giving to women the fame licentious power. The reafon they affigned was as infamous as the act; declaring that women had been too long under the tyranny of parents and of hufbands. It is not neceffary to obferve upon the horrible confequences of taking one half of the fpecies wholly out of the guardianfhip and protection of the other.

The practice of divorce, though in fome countries permitted, has been difcouraged in all. In the Eaft, polygamy and divorce are in difcredit; and the manners correct the laws. In Rome, whilft Rome was in it's integrity, the few caufes allowed for divorce amounted in effect to a prohibition. They were only three. The arbitrary was totally excluded; and accordingly fome hundreds of years paffed, without a fingle example of that kind. When manners were corrupted, the laws were relaxed; as the latter always follow the former, when they are not able to regulate them,

or

or to vanquifh them. Of this circumftance the Legiflators of vice and crime were pleafed to take
notice, as an inducement to adopt their regulation;
holding out an hope, that the permiffion would as
rarely be made ufe of. They knew the contrary to be
true ; and they had taken good care, that the laws
fhould be well feconded by the manners. Their law
of divorce, like all their laws, had not for it's object
the relief of domeftick uneafinefs, but the total
corruption of all morals, the total difconnection of
focial life.

It is a matter of curiofity to obferve the operation
of this encouragement to diforder. I have before me
the Paris paper, correfpondent to the ufual regifter
of births, marriages, and deaths. Divorce, happily, is no regular head of regiftry amongft civilized nations. With the Jacobins it is remarkable,
that divorce is not only a regular head, but it has
the poft of honour. It occupies the firft place in
the lift. In the three firft months of the year 1793,
the number of divorces in that city amounted to
562. The marriages were 1785; fo that the proportion of divorces to marriages was not much lefs than
one to three; a thing unexampled, I believe,
among mankind. I caufed an enquiry to be
made at Doctor's Commons, concerning the number of divorces; and found, that all the divorces,
(which, except by fpecial Act of Parliament, are
                                    feparations,

feparations, and not proper divorces) did not amount in all thofe Courts, and in an hundred years, to much more than one fifth of thofe that paffed, in the fingle city of Paris, in three months. I followed up the enquiry relative to that city through feveral of the fubfequent months until I was tired, and found the proportions ftill the fame. Since then I have heard that they have declared for a revifal of thefe laws: but I know of nothing done. It appears as if the contract that renovates the world was under no law at all. From this we may take our eftimate of the havock that has been made through all the relations of life. With the Ja-/cobins of France, vague intercourfe is without reproach; marriage is reduced to the vileft concubinage; children are encouraged to cut the throats of their parents; mothers are taught that tendernefs is no part of their character; and to demonftrate their attachment to their party, that they ought to make no fcruple to rake with their bloody hands in the bowels of thofe who came from their own.

To all this let us join the practice of *canniba-lifm*, with which, in the proper terms, and with the greateft truth, their feveral factions accufe each other. By cannibalifm, I mean their devouring, as a nutriment of their ferocity, fome part of the bodies of thofe they have murdered; their drinking the blood of their victims, and forcing the victims themselves to drink the blood of their kindred slaughtered before their faces. By cannibalism, I mean also to signify all their nameless, unmanly, and abominable insults on the bodies of those they slaughter.

As to those whom they suffer to die a natural death, they do not permit them to enjoy the last confolations of mankind, or those rights of sepulture, which indicate hope, and which meer nature has taught to mankind in all countries, to soothe the afflictions, and to cover the infirmity of mortal condition. They disgrace men in the entry into life ; they vitiate and enslave them through the whole course of it ; and they deprive them of all comfort at the conclusion of their dishonoured and depraved existence. Endeavouring to persuade the people that they are no better than beasts, the whole body of their institution tends to make them beasts of prey, furious and savage. For this purpose the active part of them is disciplined into a ferocity which has no parallel. To this ferocity there is joined not one of the rude, unfashioned virtues, which accompany the vices, where the whole are left to grow up together in the ranknefs of uncultivated nature. But nothing is left to nature in their systems.

The

The fame difcipline which hardens their hearts relaxes their morals. Whilft courts of juftice were thruft out by revolutionary tribunals, and filent churches were only the funeral monuments of departed religion, there were no fewer than nineteen or twenty theatres, great and fmall, moft of them kept open at the publick expence, and all of them crowded every night. Among the gaunt, hagard forms of famine and nakednefs, amidft the yells of murder, the tears of affliction, and the cries of defpair, the fong, the dance, the mimick fcene, the buffoon laughter, went on as regularly as in the gay hour of feftive peace. I have it from good authority, that under the fcaffold of judicial murder, and the gaping planks that poured down blood on the fpectators, the fpace was hired out for a fhew of dancing dogs. I think, without concert, we have made the very fame remark on reading fome of their pieces, which being written for other purpofes, let us into a view of their focial life. It ftruck us that the habits of Paris had no refemblance to the finifhed virtues, or to the polifhed vice, and elegant, though not blamelefs luxury, of the capital of a great empire. Their fociety was more like that of a den of outlaws upon a doubtful frontier ; of a lewd tavern for the revels and debauches of banditti, affaffins, bravos, fmugglers, and their more defperate paramours, mixed with bombaftick players, the refufe and rejected offal of ftrolling theatres, puffing out ill-forted verfes

about

about virtue, mixed with the licentious and blaf-
phemous fongs, proper to the brutal and hardened
courfe of life belonging to that fort of wretehes.
This fyftem of manners in itfelf is at war with all
orderly and moral fociety, and is in it's neighbourhood unfafe. If great bodies of that kind were
any where eftablifhed in a bordering territory, we
fhould have a right to demand of their Governments the fuppreffion of fuch a nuifance. What
are we to do if the Government and the whole
community is of the fame defcription? Yet that
Government has thought proper to invite ours to
lay by its unjuft hatred, and to liften to the voice
of humanity as taught by their example.

The operation of dangerous and delufive firft
principles obliges us to have recourfe to the true
ones. In the intercourfe between nations, we are
apt to rely too much on the inftrumental part.
We lay too much weight upon the formality of
treaties and compacts. We do not act much more
wifely when we truft to the interefts of men as
guarantees of their engagements. The interefts
frequently tear to pieces the engagements; and
the paffions trample upon both. Entirely to truft
to either, is to difregard our own fafety, or not to
know mankind. Men are not tied to one another by papers and feals. They are led to affo-
ciate by refemblances, by conformities, by fym-
pathies. It is with nations as with individuals.
Nothing

Nothing is fo ftrong a tie of amity between nation and nation as correfpondence in laws, cuftoms,
manners, and habits of life. They have more than
the force of treaties in themfelves. They are obligations written in the heart. They approximate
men to men, without their knowledge, and fometimes againft their intentions. The fecret, unfeen,
but irrefragable bond of habitual intercourfe, holds
them together, even when their perverfe and liti-
gious nature fets them to equivocate, fcuffle, and
fight about the terms of their written obligations.

As to war, if it be the means of wrong and violence, it is the fole means of juftice amongft nations.
Nothing can banifh it from the world. They who
fay otherwife, intending to impofe upon us, do
not impofe upon themfelves. But it is one of the
greateft objects of human wifdom to mitigate thofe
evils which we are unable to remove. The confor-
mity and analogy of which I fpeak, incapable, like
every thing elfe, of preferving perfect truft and
tranquillity among men, has a ftrong tendency
to facilitate accommodation, and to produce a generous oblivion of the rancour of their quarrels.
With this fimilitude, peace is more of peace, and
war is lefs of war. I will go further. There have
been periods of time in which communities, appa-
rently in peace with each other, have been more
perfectly feparated than, in later times, many nations

tions in Europe have been in the courſe of long
and bloody wars. The cauſe muſt be ſought in the
ſimilitude throughout Europe of religion, laws, and
manners. At bottom, theſe are all the ſame. The
writers on public law have often called this *aggregate* of nations a Commonwealth. They had reaſon. It is virtually one great ſtate having the ſame
baſis of general law; with ſome diverſity of pro-
vincial cuſtoms and local eſtabliſhments. The nations of Europe have had the very ſame chriſtian
religion, agreeing in the fundamental parts, vary-
ing a little in the ceremonies and in the ſubordi-
nate doctrines. The whole of the polity and
œconomy of every country in Europe has been
derived from the ſame ſources. It was drawn from
the old Germanic or Gothic cuſtumary; from the
feudal inſtitutions which muſt be conſidered as an
emanation from that cuſtumary; and the whole has
been improved and digeſted into ſyſtem and diſcipline by the Roman law. From hence aroſe
the ſeveral orders, with or without a Monarch,
(which are called States) in every European country; the ſtrong traces of which, where Monarchy
predominated, were never wholly extinguiſhed or
merged in deſpotiſm. In the few places where
Monarchy was caſt off, the ſpirit of European
Monarchy was ſtill left. Thoſe countriesſtill continued countries of States; that is, of claſſes, orders,
and diſtinctions, ſuch as had before ſubſiſted, or
nearly

nearly fo. Indeed the force and form of the inftitution called States, continued in greater perfection
in thofe republican communities than under Monarchies. From all thofe fcources arofe a fyftem of
manners and of education which was nearly fimilar
in all this quarter of the globe; and which foftened,
blended, and harmonized the colours of the whole.
There was little difference in the form of the
Univerfities for the education of their youth, whether with regard to faculties, to fciences, or to the
more liberal and elegant kinds of erudition. From
this refemblance in the modes of intercourfe, and in
the whole form and fafhion of life, no citizen of Europe could be altogether an exile in any part of it.
There was nothing more than a pleafing variety to
recreate and inftruct the mind ; to enrich the ima-
gina tion; and to meliorate the heart. When a man
travelled or refided for health, pleafure, bufinefs
or neceffity, from his own country, he never
felt himfelf quite abroad.

The whole body of this new fcheme of manners
in fupport of the new fcheme of politicks, I confider as a ftrong and decifive proof of determined
ambition and fyftematick hoftility. I defy the
moft refining ingenuity to invent any other caufe
for the total departure of the Jacobin Republick
from every one of the ideas and ufages, religious,
                                                    legal,

legal, moral, or focial, of this civilized world, and
for her tearing herfelf from its communion with fuch
ftudied violence, but from a formed refolution of
keeping no terms with that world. It has not been,
as has been falfely and infidioufly reprefented, that
thefe mifcreants had only broke with their old Government. They made a fchifm with the whole
univerfe; and that fchifm extended to almoft every
thing great and fmall. For one, I wifh, fince it
is gone thus far, that the breach had been fo compleat, as to make all intercourfe impracticable;
but partly by accident, partly by defign, partly
from the refiftance of the matter, enough is left to
preferve intercourfe, whilft amity is deftroyed or
corrupted in it's principle. -

This violent breach of the community of Europe, we muft conclude to have been made, (even
if they had not exprefsly declared it over and over
again) either to force mankind into an adoption
of their fyftem, or to live in perpetual enmity with
a community the moft potent we have ever known.
Can any perfon imagine, that in offering to mankind this defperate alternative, there is no indica-
tion of a hoftile mind, becaufe men in poffeffion
of the ruling authority are fuppofed to have a
right to act without coercion in their own territories? As to the right of men to act any
where according to their pleafure, without any
moral tie, no fuch right exifts. Men are never in
a ftate

a state of *total* independence of each other. It is not the condition of our nature: nor is it conceivable how any man can pursue a considerable course of action without it's having some effect upon others; or, of course, without producing some degree of responsibility for his conduct. The *situations* in which men relatively stand produce the rules and principles of that responsibility, and afford directions to prudence in exacting it.

Distance of place does not extinguish the duties or the rights of men; but it often renders their exercise impracticable. The same circumstance of distance renders the noxious effects of an evil system in any community less pernicious. But there are situations where this difficulty does not occur; and in which, therefore, these duties are obligatory, and these rights are to be asserted. It has ever been the method of publick jurists to draw a great part of the analogies on which they form the law of nations, from the principles of law which prevail in civil community. Civil laws are not all of them merely positive. Those which are rather conclusions of legal reason, than matters of statutable provision, belong to universal equity, and are universally applicable. Almost the whole prætorian law is such. There is a *Law of Neighbourhood* which does not leave a man perfect master on his own ground. When a neighbour sees a *new erection*,

Q

in the nature of a nuifance, fet up at his door, he
has a right to reprefent it to the judge; who, on his
part, has a right to order the work to be ftaid; or if
eftablifhed, to be removed. On this head, the parent
law is exprefs and clear; and has made many wife
provifions, which, without deftroying, regulate and
reftrain the right of *ownerfhip*, by the right of *vi-
tinage*. No *innovation* is permitted that may re-
dound, even fecondarily, to the prejudice of a
neighbour. The whole doctrine of that important
head of prætorian law, " *De novi operis nunciatione*,"
is founded on the principle, that no *new* ufe fhould
be made of a man's private liberty of operating
upon his private property, from whence a detriment
may be juftly apprehended by his neighbour.
This law of denunciation is profpective. It is
to anticipate what is called *damnum infectum*, or
damnum nondum factum, that is a damage juftly
apprehended but not actually done. Even before
it is clearly known, whether the innovation be da-
mageable or not, the judge is competent to iffue a
prohibition to innovate, until the point can be determined. This prompt interference is grounded
on principles favourable to both parties. It is pre-
ventive of mifchief difficult to be repaired, and of
ill blood difficult to be foftened. The rule of
law, therefore, which comes before the evil, is
amongft the very beft parts of equity, and juftifies
the promptnefs of the remedy; becaufe, as it is well
observed,

obferved, *Res damni infecti celeritatem defiderat & periculofa eft dilatio.* This right of denunciation does not hold, when things continue, however inconveniently to the neighbourhood, according to the *antient* mode. For there is a fort of prefumption againft novelty, drawn out of a deep confideration of human nature and human affairs; and the maxim of jurifprudence is well laid down, *Vetuftas pro lege femper habetur.*

Such is the law of civil vicinity. Now where there is no conftituted judge, as between independent ftates there is not, the vicinage itfelf is the natural judge. It is, preventively, the affertor of it's own rights; or remedially, their avenger. Neighbours are prefumed to take cognizance of each other's acts. " *Vicini, vicinorum facta prefumuntur fcire.*" This principle, which, like the reft, is as true of nations, as of individual men, has beftowed on the grand vicinage of Europe, a duty to know, and a right to prevent, any capital innovation which may amount to the erection of a dangerous nuifance.* Of the importance of that innovation, and the

---

* " This ftate of things cannot exift in France without in-
" volving all the furrounding powers in one common danger,
" without giving them the right, without impofing it on them
" as a duty, to ftop the progrefs of an evil which attacks the fun-
" damental principles by which mankind is united in civil fo-
" ciety." Declaration, 29th Oct. 1793.

Q 2   mifchief

mifchief of that nuifance, they are, to be fure,
bound to judge not litigioufly : but it is in their
competence to judge. They have uniformly
acted on this right. What in civil fociety is a
ground of action, in politick fociety is a ground of
war. But the exercife of that competent jurifdiction is a matter of moral prudence. As fuits in
civil fociety, fo war in the political muft ever be a
matter of great deliberation. It is not this or
that particular proceeding, picked out here and
there, as a fubject of quarrel, that will do.
There muft be an aggregate of mifchief. There
muft be marks of deliberation ; there muft be
traces of defign ; there muft be indications of
malice; there muft be tokens of ambition. There
muft be force in the body where they exift ; there
muft be energy in the mind. When all thefe circumftances combine, or the important parts of
them, the duty of the vicinity calls for the exercife
of it's competence ; and the rules of prudence do
not reftrain, but demand it.

In defcribing the nuifance erected by fo peftilential a manufactory, by the conftruction of fo infamous a brothel, by digging a night cellar for fuch
thieves, murderers, and houfe-breakers, as never in-
fefted the world, I am fo far from aggravating, that
I have fallen infinitely fhort of the evil. No man
who has attended to the particulars of what has
been

been done in France, and combined them with
the principles there afferted, can poffibly doubt it.
When I compare with this great caufe of nations,
the trifling points of honour, the ftill more con-
temptible points of intereft, the light ceremonies,
the undefinable punctilios, the difputes about pre-
cedency, the lowering or the hoifting of a fail, the
dealing in a hundred or two of wild cat-fkins on
the other fide of the Globe, which have often
kindled up the flames of war between nations, I
ftand aftonifhed at thofe perfons, who do not feel
a refentment, not more natural than politick, at
the atrocious infults that this monftrous com-
pound offers to the dignity of every nation, and
who are not alarmed with what it threatens to their
fafety.

I have therefore been decidedly of opinion, with
our declaration at Whitehall, in the beginning of this
war, that the vicinage of Europe had not only a right,
but an indifpenfible duty, and an exigent intereft,
to denunciate this new work before it had produced
the danger we have fo forely felt, and which we
fhall long feel. The example of what is done by
France is too important not to have a vaft and
extenfive influence; and that example backed with
it's power, muft bear with great force on thofe
who are near it; efpecially on thofe who fhall recognize the pretended Republick on the principle
upon

upon which it now ſtands. It is not an old ſtruc-
ture which you have found as it is, and are not
to diſpute of the original end and deſign with
which it had been ſo faſhioned. It is a recent
wrong, and can plead no preſcription. It violates
the rights upon which not only the community of
France, but thoſe on which all communities are
founded. The principles on which they proceed
are *general* principles, and are as true in England
as in any other country. They who (though
with the pureſt intentions) recognize the authority of theſe Regicides and robbers upon principle, juſtify their acts, and eſtabliſh them as pre-
cedents. It is a queſtion not between France and
England. It is a queſtion between property and
force. The property claims ; and it's claim has
been allowed. The property of the nation is the
nation. They who maſſacre, plunder, and expel
the body of the proprietary, are murderers and robbers. The State, in it's eſſence, muſt be moral
and juſt : and it may be ſo, though a tyrant or
uſurper ſhould be accidentally at the head of it.
This is a thing to be lamented: but this not-
withſtanding, the body of the commonwealth
may remain in all it's integrity and be perfectly
ſound in it's compoſition. The preſent caſe is
different. It is not a revolution in government.
It is not the victory of party over party. It is a de-
ſtruction and decompoſition of the whole ſociety ;
which

which never can be made of right by any faction,
however powerful, nor without terrible confequences
to all about it, both in the act and in the example.
This pretended Republick is founded in crimes, and
exifts by wrong and robbery; and wrong and robbery, far from a title to any thing, is war with
mankind. To be at peace with robbery is to be
an accomplice with it.

Mere locality does not conftitute a body politick. Had Cade and his gang got poffeffion of
London, they would not have been the Lord-
Mayor, Aldermen, and Common Council. The
body politick of France exifted in the majefty
of it's throne; in the dignity of it's nobility;
in the honour of it's gentry; in the fanctity of it's
clergy; in the reverence of it's magiftracy; in
the weight and confideration due to it's landed
property in the feveral bailliages; in the refpect
due to it's moveable fubftance reprefented by
the corporations of the kingdom. All thefe particular *molecula* united, form the great mafs
of what is truly the body politick in all countries. They are fo many depofits and recep-
tacles of juftice; becaufe they can only exift
by juftice. Nation is a moral effence, not a geo-
graphical arrangement, or a denomination of
the nomenclator. France, though out of her
territorial poffeffion, exifts; becaufe the fole

poffible claimant, I mean the proprietary, and the government to which the proprietary ad heres, exifts and claims. God forbid, that if you were expelled from your houfe by ruffians and affaffins, that I fhould call the material walls, doors and windows of ———, the ancient and honourable family of ———. Am I to transfer to the intruders, who not content to turn you out naked to the world, would rob you of your very name, all the efteem and refpect I owe to you? The Regicides in France are not France. France is out of her bounds, but the kingdom is the fame.

To illuftrate my opinions on this fubject, let us fuppofe a cafe, which, after what has happened, we cannot think abfolutely impoffible, though the augury is to be abominated, and the event deprecated with our moft ardent prayers. Let us fuppofe then, that our gracious Sovereign was facrilegiously murdered; his exemplary Queen, at the head of the matronage of this land, murdered in the fame manner: That thofe Princeffes whofe beauty and modeft elegance are the ornaments of the country, and who are the leaders and patterns of the ingenuous youth of their fex, were put to a cruel and ignominious death, with hundreds of others, mothers and daughters, ladies of the firft diftinction;---that the Prince of Wales and the Duke of York, princes the hope and pride of the nation,

nation, with all their brethren, were forced to fly from the knives of affaffins---that the whole body of our excellent Clergy were either maffacred or robbed of all, and tranfported—the Chriftian Religion, in all it's denominations, forbidden and perfecuted; the law totally, fundamentally, and in all it's parts deftroyed—the judges put to death by revolutionary tribunals--the Peers and Commons robbed to the laft acre of their eftates; maffacred if they ftaid, or obliged to feek life in flight, in exile and in beggary—that the whole landed property fhould fhare the very fame fate—that every military and naval officer of honour and rank, almoft to a man, fhould be placed in the fame defcription of confifcation and exile—that the principal merchants and bankers fhould be drawn out, as from an hen-coop, for flaughter—that the citizens of our greateft and moft flourifhing cities, when the hand and the machinery of the hangman were not found fufficient, fhould have been collected in the publick fquares, and maffacred by thoufands with cannon ;—if three hundred thoufand others fhould have been doomed to a fituation worfe than death in noifome and peftilential prifons;—in fuch a cafe, is it in the faction of robbers I am to look for my country? Would this be the England that you and I, and even ftrangers, admired, honoured, loved, and cherifhed? Would not the exiles of England alone be my Government and my fellow citizens? Would

R   not

not their places of refuge be my temporary country?
Would not all my duties and all my affections be
there and there only? Should I confider myfelf as a
traitor to my country, and deferving of death, if I
knocked at the door and heart of every Potentate
in Chriftendom to fuccour my friends, and to
avenge them on their enemies? Could I, in any
way, fhew myfelf more a Patriot? What fhould
I think of thofe Potentates who infulted their
fuffering brethren; who treated them as vagrants,
or at leaft as mendicants; and could find no
allies, no friends, but in Regicide murderers
and robbers? What ought I to think and feel,
if being geographers inftead of Kings, they recognized the defolated cities, the wafted fields,
and the rivers polluted with blood, of this geo-
metrical meafurement, as the honourable member
of Europe, called England? In that condition
what fhould we think of Sweden, Denmark, or
Holland, or whatever Power afforded us a churlifh
and treacherous hofpitality, if they fhould invite
us to join the ftandard of our King, our Laws,
and our Religion, if they fhould give us a direct
promife of protection,---if after all this, taking advantage of our deplorable fituation, which left us
no choice, they were to treat us as the loweft and
vileft of all mercenaries? If they were to fend us
far from the aid of our King, and our fuffering
Country, to fquander us away in the moft peftilential

tial climates for a venal enlargement of their own
territories, for the purpofe of trucking them, when
obtained, with thofe very robbers and murderers
they had called upon us to oppofe with our blood?
What would be our fentiments, if in that miferable fervice we were not to be confidered either as
Englifh, ór as Swedes, Dutch, Danes, but as out-
cafts of the human race? Whilft we were fighting
thofe battles of their intereft, and as their foldiers,
how fhould we feel if we were to be excluded
from all their cartels? How muft we feel, if the
pride and flower of the Englifh Nobility and
Gentry, who might efcape the peftilential clime,
and the devouring fword, fhould, if taken pri-
foners, be delivered over as rebel fubjects, to be
condemned as rebels, as traitors, as the vileft of
all criminals, by tribunals formed of Maroon ne-
groe flaves, covered over with the blood of their
mafters, who were made free and organifed into
judges, for their robberies and murders? What fhould
we feel under this inhuman, infulting, and barbarous
protection of Mufcovites, Swedes or Hollanders?
Should we not obteft Heaven, and whatever juftice
there is yet on Earth? Oppreffion makes wife men
mad; but the diftemper is ftill the madnefs of the
wife, which is better than the fobriety of fools.
Their cry is the voice of facred mifery, exalted, not
into wild raving, but into the fanctified phrenfy
of prophecy and infpiration---in that bitternefs of

R 2   foul,

foul, in that indignation of suffering virtue, in that exaltation of despair, would not persecuted English Loyalty cry out, with an awful warning voice, and denounce the destruction that waits on Monarchs, who consider fidelity to them as the most degrading of all vices; who suffer it to be punished as the most abominable of all crimes; and who have no respect but for rebels, traitors, Regicides, and furious negro slaves, whose crimes have broke their chains? Would not this warm language of high indignation have more of sound reason in it, more of real affection, more of true attachment, than all the lullabies of flatterers, who would hush Monarchs to sleep in the arms of death? Let them be well convinced, that if ever this example should prevail in it's whole extent, it will have it's full operation. Whilst Kings stand firm on their base, though under that base there is a sure-wrought mine, there will not be wanting to their levees a single person of those who are attached to their fortune, and not to their persons or cause: But hereafter none will support a tottering throne. Some will fly for fear of being crushed under the ruin; some will join in making it. They will seek in the destruction of Royalty, fame, and power, and wealth, and the homage of Kings, with *Reubel*, with *Carnot*, with *Revelliere*, and with the *Merlins* and the *Talliens*, rather than suffer exile and beggary with the *Condés*, or the *Broglios*,

the

the *Caſtries*, the *D'Avrais*, the *Serrents*, the *Ca-*
zalés, and the long line of loyal, fuffering Patriot
Nobility, or to be butchered with the oracles and
the victims of the laws, the *D'Ormeſtons*, the *d'Eſ-*
premenils, and the *Maleſherbes*. This example we
fhall give, if inſtead of adhering to our fellows in a
caufe which is an honour to us all, we abandon the
lawful Government and lawful corporate body of
France, to hunt for a fhameful and ruinous fraternity, with this odious ufurpation that difgraces civilized fociety and the human race,

And is then example nothing? It is every thing.
Example is the fchool of mankind, and they will
learn at no other. This war is a war againſt that
example. It is not a war for Louis the Eighteenth,
or even for the property, virtue, fidelity of France.
It is a war for George the Third, for Francis the
Second, and for all the dignity, property, honour,
virtue, and religion of England, of Germany, and
of all nations.

I know that all I have faid of the fyſtematick
unfociability of this new-invented fpecies of republick, and the impoffibility of preferving peace, is an-
fwered by afferting that the fcheme of manners, morals, and even of maxims and principles of ſtate, is
of no weight in a queſtion of peace or war between
communities. This doctrine is fupported by example.

ample. The cafe of Algiers is cited, with an hint, as if it were the ftronger cafe. I fhould take no notice of this fort of inducement, if I had found it only where firft it was. I do not want refpect for thofe from whom I firft heard it—but having no controverfy at prefent with them, I only think it not amifs to reft on it a little, as I find it adopted with much more of the fame kind, by feveral of thofe on whom fuch reafoning had formerly made no apparent impreffion. If it had no force to prevent us from fubmitting to this neceffary war, it furnifhes no better ground for our making an unneceffary and ruinous peace.

This analogical argument drawn from the cafe of Algiers would lead us a good way. The fact is, we ourfelves with a little cover, others more directly, pay a *tribute* to the Republick of Algiers. Is it meant to reconcile us to the payment of a *tribute* to the French Republick? That this, with other things more ruinous, will be demanded hereafter, I little doubt; but for the prefent, this will not be avowed---though our minds are to be gradually prepared for it. In truth, the arguments from this cafe are worth little, even to thofe who approve the buying an Algerine forbearance of piracy. There are many things which men do not approve, that they muft do to avoid a greater evil. To argue from thence, that they are

are to act in the fame manner in all cafes, is
turning neceffity into a law. Upon what is matter of prudence, the argument concludes the contrary way. Becaufe we have done one humiliating act, we ought, with infinite caution, to admit
more acts of the fame nature, left humiliation
fhould become our habitual ftate. Matters of prudence are under the dominion of circumftances,
and not of logical analogies. It is fo abfurd to take
it otherwife.

I, for one, do more than doubt the policy of
this kind of convention with Algiers. On thofe
who think as I do, the argument *ad hominem* can
make no fort of impreffion. I know fomething of
the Conftitution and compofition of this very extraordinary Republick. It has a Conftitution, I admit,
fimilar to the prefent tumultuous military tyranny
of France, by which an handful of obfcure ruffians
domineer over a fertile country, and a brave people.
For the compofition, too, I admit, the Algerine
community refembles that of France; being formed out of the very fcum, fcandal, difgrace, and peft
of the Turkifh Afia. The grand Seignor, to difbur-
then the country, fuffers the Dey to recruit, in his
dominions, the corps of Janifaries, or Afaphs, which
form the Directory and Council of Elders of the
African Republick one and indivifible. But
notwithftanding this refemblance, which I allow, I
never

never shall so far injure the Janisarian Republick of Algiers, as to put it in comparison for every sort of crime, turpitude, and oppression with the Jacobin Republick of Paris. There is no question with me to which of the two I should choose to be a neighbour or a subject. But situated as I am, I am in no danger of becoming to Algiers either the one or the other. It is not so in my relation to the atheistical fanaticks of France. I *am* their neighbour; I *may* become their subject. Have the Gentlemen who borrowed this happy parallel, no idea of the different conduct to be held with regard to the very same evil at an immense distance, and when it is at your door? when it's power is enormous, as when it is comparatively as feeble as it's distance is remote? when there is a barrier of language and usages, which prevents corruption through certain old correspondences and habitudes, from the contagion of the horrible novelties that are introduced into every thing else? I can contemplate, without dread, a royal or a national tyger on the borders of Pegu. I can look at him, with an easy curiosity, as prisoner within bars in the menagerie of the Tower. But if, by Habeas Corpus, or otherwise, he was to come into the Lobby of the House of Commons whilst your door was open, any of you would be more stout than wife, who would not gladly make your escape out of the back windows. I certainly
                                    should

fhould dread more from a wild cat in my bed-
chamber, than from all the lions that roar in the
deferts behind Algiers. But in this parallel it is
the cat that is at a diftance, and the lions and ty-
gers that are in our anti-chambers and our lobbies.
Algiers is not near; Algiers is not powerful; Algiers is not our neighbour; Algiers is not infec-
tious. Algiers, whatever it may be, is an old crea-
tion; and we have good data to calculate all the
mifchief to be apprehended from it. When I find
Algiers transferred to Calais, I will tell you what I
think of that point. In the mean time, the cafe
quoted from the Algerine reports, will not apply
as authority. We fhall put it out of court; and
fo far as that goes, let the counfel for the Jacobin
peace take nothing by their motion.

When we voted, as you and I did, with many
more whom you and I refpect and love, to refift
this enemy, we were providing for dangers that were
direct, home, prefling, and not remote, contingent,
uncertain, and formed upon loofe analogies. We
judged of the danger with which we were menaced by
Jacobin F.ance, from the whole tenor of it's conduct;
not from one or two doubtful or detached acts or
expreffions. I not only concurred in the idea of
combining with Europe in this war; but to the
beft of my power ever ftimulated Minifters to that
conjunction of interefts and of efforts. I joined
S   with

with them with all my foul, on the principles contained in that manly and mafterly ftate-paper,
which I have two or three times referred to,* and
may ftill more frequently hereafter. The diplomatick collection never was more enriched than with
this piece. The hiftorick facts juftify every ftroke
of the mafter. " Thus painters write their names
at Co."

Various perfons may concur in the fame meafure on various grounds. They may be various,
without being contrary to, or exclufive of each
other. I thought the infolent, unprovoked aggreffion of the Regicide, upon our Ally of Holland, a good ground of war. I think his manifeft
attempt to overturn the balance of Europe, a
good ground of war. As a good ground of war,
I confider his declaration of war on his Majefty
and his kingdom. But though I have taken all
thefe to my aid, I confider them as nothing
more than as a fort of evidence to indicate the
treafonable mind within. Long before their acts
of aggreffion, and their declaration of war, the
faction in France had affumed a form, had adopted a body of principles and maxims, and had regularly and fyftematically acted on them, by which
fhe virtually had put herfelf in a pofture, which
was in itfelf a declaration of war againft mankind.

* Declaration, Whitehall, Oct, 29, 1793.

It

It is: said by the Directory in their feveral manifeftoes, that we of the people are tumultuous for
peace ; and that Minifters pretend negociation to
amufe us. This they have learned from the language of many amongft ourfelves, whofe converfations have been one main caufe of whatever extent
the opinion for peace with Regicide may be. But
I who think the Minifters unfortunately to be but
too ferious in their proceedings, find myfelf obliged
to fay a little more on this fubject of the popular
opinion.

Before our opinions are quoted againft ourfelves,
it is proper that, from our ferious deliberation, they
may be worth quoting. It is without reafon we
praife the wifdom of our Conftitution, in putting under the difcretion of the Crown, the awful truft of
war and peace, if the Minifters of the Crown
virtually return it again into our hands. The truft
was placed there as a facred depofit, to fecure us
againft popular rafhnefs in plunging into wars,
and againft the effects of popular difmay, difguft, or laffitude in getting out of them as im-
prudently as we might firft engage in them. To
have no other meafure in judging of thofe great objects than our momentary opinions and defires, is
to throw us back upon that very democracy which,
in this part, our Conftitution was formed to avoid.

It

It is no excuse at all for a minister, who at our desire, takes a measure contrary to our safety, that it is our own act. He who does not stay the hand of suicide, is guilty of murder. On our part I say, that to be instructed, is not to be degraded or enslaved. Information is an advantage to us; and we have a right to demand it. He that is bound to act in the dark cannot be said to act freely. When it appears evident to our governors that our desires and our interests are at variance, they ought not to gratify the former at the expence of the latter. Statesmen are placed on an eminence, that they may have a larger horizon than we can possibly command. They have a whole before them, which we can contemplate only in the parts, and even without the necessary relations. Ministers are not only our natural rulers but our natural guides. Reason clearly and manfully delivered, has in itself a mighty force: but reason in the mouth of legal authority, is, I may fairly say, irresistible.

I admit that reason of state will not, in many circumstances permit the disclosure of the true ground of a public proceeding. In that case silence is manly and it is wise. It is fair to call for trust when the principle of reason itself suspends it's public use. I take the distinction to be this. The ground of a particular measure, making a part of a plan, a plan, it is rarely proper to divulge. All the broader grounds of policy on which the general plan is to be adopted, ought as rarely to be concealed. They who have not the whole cause before them, call them politicians, call them people, call them what you will, are no judges. The difficulties of the cafe, as well as it's fair fide, ought to be prefented. This ought to be done: and it is all that can be done. When we have our true fituation diftinctly prefented to us, if then we refolve with a blind and headlong violence, to refift the admonitions of our friends, and to caft ourfelves into the hands of our potent and irreconcileable foes, then, and not till then, the minifters ftand acquitted before God and man, for whatever may come.

Lamenting as I do, that the matter has not had fo full and free a difcuffion as it requires, I mean to omit none of the points which feem to me neceffary for confideration, previous to an arrangement which is for ever to decide the form and the fate of Europe. In the courfe, therefore, of what I fhall have the honour to addrefs to you, I propofe the following queftions to your ferious thoughts. 1. Whether the prefent fyftem, which ftands for a Government in France, be fuch as in peace and war affects the neighbouring States in a manner different from the internal Government

ment that formerly prevailed in that country?
2. Whether that syftem, suppofing it's views hoftile
to other nations, poffeffes any means of being
hurtful to them peculiar to itfelf? 3. Whether
there has been lately fuch a change in France,
as to alter the nature of it's fyftem, or it's effect
upon other Powers? 4. Whether any publick declarations or engagements exift, on the part of the
allied Powers, which ftand in the way of a treaty
of peace, which fuppofes the right and confirms
the power of the Regicide faction in France?
5. What the ftate of the other Powers of Europe
will be with refpect to each other, and their colonies,
on the conclufion of a Regicide Peace? 6. Whether we are driven to the abfolute neceffity of
making that kind of peace?

Thefe heads of enquiry will enable us to make
the application of the feveral matters of fact and
topicks of argument, that occur in this vaft difcuffion, to certain fixed principles. I do not
mean to confine myfelf to the order in which they
ftand. I fhall difcufs them in fuch a manner as
fhall appear to me the beft adapted for fhewing
their mutual bearings and relations. Here then I
clofe the public matter of my Letter; but before
I have done, let me fay one word in apology for
myfelf.

In

In wifhing this nominal peace not to be precipi-
tated, I am fure no man living is lefs difpofed to
blame the prefent Miniftry than I am. Some of
my oldeft friends, (and I wifh I could fay it of
more of them) make a part in that Miniftry.
There are fome indeed, "whom my dim eyes in vain
explore." In my mind, a greater calamity could
not have fallen on the publick than the exclufion
of one of them. But I drive away that, with other
melancholy thoughts. A great deal ought to be faid
upon that fubject or nothing. As to the diftinguifhed
perfons to whom my friends who remain, are joined,
if benefits, nobly and generoufly conferred, ought
to procure good wifhes, they are intitled to my
beft vows; and they have them all. They have
adminiftered to me the. only confolation I am
capable of receiving, which is to know that no
individual will fuffer by my thirty years fervice
to the publick. If things fhould give us the com-
parative happinefs of a ftruggle, I fhall be found,
I was going to fay fighting, (that would - be
foolifh) but dying by the fide of Mr. Pitt. I muft
add, that if any thing defenfive in our domeftick
fyftem can poffibly fave us from the difafters of a
Regicide peace, he is the man to fave us. If the
finances in fuch a cafe can be repaired, he is
the man to repair them. If I fhould lament any
of his acts, it is only when they appear to me
to have no refemblance to acts of his. But

let

let him not have a confidence in himfelf, which no human abilities can warrant. His abilities are fully equal (and that is to fay much for any man) to thofe that are oppofed to him. But if we look to him as our fecurity againft the confequences of a Regicide Peace, let us be affured, that a Regicide Peace and a Conftitutional Miniftry are terms that will not agree. With a Regicide Peace the King cannot long have a Minifter to ferve him, nor the Minifter a King to ferve. If the Great Difpofer, in reward of the royal and the private virtues of our Sovereign, fhould call him from the calamitous fpectacles, which will attend a ftate of amity with Regicide, his fucceffor will furely fee them, unlefs the fame Providence greatly anticipates the courfe of nature. Thinking thus, (and not, as I conceive, on light grounds) I dare not flatter the reigning Sovereign, nor any Minifter he has or can have, nor his Succeffor Apparent, nor any of thofe who may be called to ferve him, with what appears to me a falfe ftate of their fituation. We cannot have them and that Peace together.

I do not forget that there had been a confiderable difference between feveral of our friends, with my infignificant felf, and the great man at the head of Miniftry, in an early ftage of thefe difcuffions. But I am fure there was a period in which we agreed better in the danger of a Jacobin exift-

ence

ence in France. At one time, he and all Europe
feemed to feel it. But why am not I converted
with fo many great Powers, and fo many great
Minifters ? It is because I am old and flow,——
I am in this year, 1796, only where all the powers
of Europe were in 1793. I cannot move with this
proceffion of the Equinoxes, which is preparing for us
the return of fome very old, I am afraid no golden
æra, or the commencement of fome new æra that
must be denominated from fome new metal. In
this crifis I muft hold my tongue, or I muft fpeak
with freedom. Falfhood and delufion are allowed
in no cafe whatever : But, as in the exercife of all
the virtues, there is an œconomy of truth. It is a
fort of temperance, by which a man fpeaks truth
with meafure that he may fpeak it the longer. But
as the fame rules do not hold in all cafes—what
would be right for you, who may prefume on a
feries of years before you, would have no fenfe for
me, who cannot, without abfurdity, calculate on
fix months of life. What I fay, I *muft* fay at once.
Whatever I write is in it's nature teftamentary. It
may have the weaknefs, but it has the fincerity of
a dying declaration. For the few days I have to
linger here, I am removed completely from the
bufy fcene of the world; but I hold myfelf to be
ftill refponfible for every thing that I have done
whilft I continued on the place of action. If the
raweft Tyro in politicks has been influenced by the

T   authority

authority of my grey hairs, and led by any thing in my fpeeches, or my writings, to enter into this war, he has a right to call upon me to know why I have changed my opinions, or why, when thofe I voted with, have adopted better notions, I perfevere in exploded errour?

When I feem not to acquiefce in the acts of thofe I refpect in every degree fhort of fuperftition, I am obliged to give my reafons fully. I cannot fet my authority againft their authority. But to exert reafon is not to revolt againft authority. Reafon and authority do not move in the fame parallel. That reafon is an *amicus curiæ* who fpeaks *de plano*, not *pro tribunali*. It is a friend who makes an ufeful fuggeftion to the Court, without queftioning it's jurifdiction. Whilft he acknowledges it's competence, he promotes it's efficiency. I fhall purfue the plan I have chalked out in my Letters that follow this.

LETTER

LETTER II.

*On the Genius and Character of the French
Revolution as it regards other Nations.*

MY DEAR SIR,

I Clofed my firft Letter with ferious matter;
and I hope it has employed your thoughts.
The fyftem of peace muft have a reference to
the fyftem of the war. On that ground, I muft
therefore again recal your mind to our original
opinions, which time and events have not
taught me to vary.

My ideas and my principles led me, in this
conteft, to encounter France, not as a State, but
as a Faction. The vaft territorial extent of that
country, it's immenfe population, it's riches of
production, it's riches of commerce and convention—the whole aggregate mafs of what, in
ordinary cafes, conftitutes the force of a State,
to me were but objects of fecondary confideration. They might be balanced; and they have

T 2   been

been often more than balanced. Great as thefe things are, they are not what make the faction formidable. It is the faction that makes them truly dreadful. That faction is the evil fpirit that poffeffes the body of France; that informs it as a foul; that ftamps upon it's ambition, and upon all it's purfuits, a characteriftick mark, which ftrongly diftinguifhes them from the fame general paffions, and the fame general views, in other men and in other communities. It is that fpirit which infpires into them, a new, a pernicious, a defolating activity. Conftituted as France was ten years ago, it was not in that France to fhake, to fhatter, and to overwhelm Europe in the manner that we behold. A fure deftruction impends over thofe infatuated Princes, who, in the conflict with this new and unheard-of power, proceed as if they were engaged in a war that bore a refemblance to their former contefts; or that they can make peace in the fpirit of their former arrangements of pacification. Here the beaten path is the very reverfe of the fafe road.

As to me, I was always fteadily of opinion, that this diforder was not in it's nature intermittent. I conceived that the conteft once begun, could not be laid down again, to be refumed at our difcretion; but that our

firft

firſt ſtruggle with this evil would alſo be our
laſt. I never thought we could make peace
with the ſyſtem; becauſe it was not for the ſake
of an object we purſued in rivalry with each
other, but with the ſyſtem itſelf that we were at
war. As I underſtood the matter, we were at
war not with it's conduct, but with it's exiſtence; convinced that it's exiſtence and it's hoſ-
tility were the ſame.

The faction is not local or territorial. It is a
general evil. Where it leaſt appears in action,
it is ſtill full of life. In it's ſleep it recruits it's
ſtrength, and prepares it's exertion. It's ſpirit lies
deep in the corruptions of our common nature.
The ſocial order which reſtrains it, feeds it. It
exiſts in every country in Europe; and among
all orders of men in every country, who look up
to France as to a common head. The centre is
there. The circumference is the world of Europe wherever the race of Europe may be ſettled. Every where elſe the faction is militant; in
France it is triumphant. In France is the bank
of depoſit, and the bank of circulation, of all
the pernicious principles that are forming in
every State. It will be a folly ſcarcely deſerving
of pity, and too miſchievous for contempt, to
think of reſtraining it in any other country
whilſt it is predominant there. War, inſtead of
being

being the caufe of it's force, has fufpended it's operation. It has given a reprieve, at leaft, to the Chriftian World.

The true nature of a Jacobin war, in the beginning, was, by moft of the Chriftian Powers, felt, acknowledged, and even in the moft precife manner declared. In the joint manifefto, publifhed by the Emperor and the King of Pruffia, on the 4th of Auguft 1792, it is expreffed in the cleareft terms, and on principles which could not fail, if they had adhered to them, of claffing thofe monarchs with the firft benefactors of mankind. This manifefto was publifhed, as they themfelves exprefs it, " to " lay open to the prefent generation, as well as " to pofterity, their motives, their intentions, " and the *difintereftednefs* of their perfonal views; " taking up arms for the purpofe of preferving " focial and political order amongft all civilized " nations, and to fecure to *each* ftate it's reli- " gion, happinefs, independence, territories, " and real conftitution."—" On this ground, " they hoped that all Empires, and all States, " ought to be unanimous; and becoming the firm " guardians of the happinefs of mankind, that " they cannot fail to unite their efforts to refcue " a numerous nation from it's own fury, to pre- " ferve Europe from the return of barbarifm, " and

" and the Univerfe from the fubverfion and
" anarchy with which it was threatened." The
whole of that noble performance ought to be read
at the firft meeting of any Congrefs, which may
affemble for the purpofe of pacification. In that
piece " thefe Powers exprefsly renounce all views
" of perfonal aggrandizement," and confine
themfelves to objects worthy of fo generous, fo
heroic, and fo perfectly wife and politick an enterprife. It was to the principles of this confe-
deration and to no other, that we wifhed our
Sovereign and our Country to accede, as a part
· of the commonwealth of Europe. To thefe
principles with fome trifling exceptions and
limitations they did fully accede.* And all our
friends who did take office acceded to the Miniftry (whether wifely or not) as I always underftood the matter, on the faith and on the
principles of that declaration.

As long as thefe powers flattered themfelves
that the menace of force would produce the effect of force, they acted on thofe declarations;
but when their menaces failed of fuccefs, their
efforts took a new direction. It did not appear
to them that virtue and heroifm ought to be purchafed by millions of rix-dollars. It is a dreadful

* See Declaration, Whitehall, Oct. 29, 1793.

truth,

truth, but it is a truth that cannot be concealed; in ability, in dexterity, in the diftinctnefs of their views, the Jacobins are our fuperiours. They faw the thing right from the very beginning. What-.ever were the firft motives to the war among politicians, they faw that it is in it's fpirit, and for it's objects, a *civil war*; and as fuch they purfued it. It is a war between the partizans of the antient, civil, moral, and political order of Europe againft a fect of fanatical and ambitious atheifts which means to change them all. It is not France extending a foreign empire over other nations : it is a fect aiming at univerfal empire, and beginning with the conqueft of France. The leaders of that fect fecured the *centre of Europe*; and that fecured, they knew, that whatever might be the event of battles and fieges, their *caufe* was victorious. Whether it's territory had a little more or a little lefs peeled from it's furface, or whether an ifland or two was detached from it's commerce, to them was of little moment. The conqueft of France was a glorious acquifition. That once well laid as a bafis of empire, opportunities never could be wanting to regain or to replace what had been loft, and dreadfully to avenge themfelves on the faction of their adverfaries.

They

They faw it was a *civil war*. It was their bufinefs to perfuade their adverfaries that it ought
to be a *foreign* war. The Jacobins every where
fet up a cry againft the new crufade ; and they
intrigued with effect in the cabinet, in the field,
and in every private fociety in Europe. Their
tafk was not difficult. The condition of Princes,
and fometimes of firft Minifters too, is to
be pitied. The creatures of the defk, and
the creatures of favour, had no relifh for
the principles of the manifeftoes. They promifed no governments, no regiments, no reve-
nues from whence emoluments might arife, by
perquifite or by grant. In truth, the tribe of
vulgar politicians are the loweft of our fpecies.
There is no trade fo vile and mechanical as government in their hands. Virtue is not their
habit. They are out of themfelves in any courfe
of conduct recommended only by confcience
and glory. A large, liberal and profpective
view of the interefts of States paffes with them
for romance ; and the principles that recom-
mend it for the wanderings of a difordered
imagination. The calculators compute them
out of their fenfes. The jefters and buffoons
fhame them out of every thing grand and elevated. Littlenefs in object and in means, to
them appears foundnefs and fobriety. They think
there is nothing worth purfuit, but that which

U   they

they can handle; which they can measure with a two-foot rule; which they can tell upon ten fingers.

Without the principles of the Jacobins, perhaps without any principles at all, they played the game of that faction. There was a beaten road before them. The Powers of Europe were armed; France had always appeared dangerous; the war was easily diverted from France as a faction, to France as a state. The Princes were easily taught to slide back into their old habitual course of politicks. They were easily led to consider the flames that were consuming France, not as a warning to protect their own buildings, (which were without any party wall, and linked by a contignation into the edifice of France,) as an happy occasion for pillaging the goods, and for carrying off the materials of their neighbour's house. Their provident fears were changed into avaricious hopes. They carried on their new designs without seeming to abandon the principles of their old policy. They pretended to seek, or they flattered themselves that they sought, in the accession of new fortresses, and new territories, a *defensive* security. But the security wanted was against a kind of power, which was not so truly dangerous in it's fortresses nor in it's territories, as in it's spirit and it's it's principles. They aimed, or pretended to aim, at *defending* themselves againſt a danger, from which there can be no ſecurity in any *defenſive* plan. If armies and fortreſſes were a defence againſt Jacobiniſm, Louis the Sixteenth would this day reign a powerful monarch over an happy people.

This error obliged them, even in their offenſive operations, to adopt a plan of war, againſt the ſucceſs of which there was ſomething little ſhort of mathematical demonſtration. They refuſed to take any ſtep which might ſtrike at the heart of affairs. They ſeemed unwilling to wound the enemy in any vital part. They acted through the whole, as if they really wiſhed the conſervation of the Jacobin power; as what might be more favourable than the lawful Government to the attainment of the petty objects they looked for. They always kept on the circumference; and the wider and remoter the circle was, the more eagerly they choſe it as their ſphere of action in this centrifugal war. The plan they purſued, in it's nature demanded great length of time. In it's execution, they, who went the neareſt way to work, were obliged to cover an incredible extent of country. It left to the enemy every means of deſtroying this extended line of weakneſs. Ill ſucceſs in any part was ſure to de-

feat

feat the effect of the whole. This is true of Auftria. It is ftill more true of England. On this
falfe plan, even good fortune, by further weak-
ening the victor, put him but the further off
from his object.

As long as there was any appearance of fuccefs, the fpirit of aggrandizement, and confequently the fpirit of mutual jealoufy feized upon
all the coalefced Powers. Some fought an acceffion of territory at the expence of France,
fome at the expence of each other; fome at the
expence of third parties; and when the viciffi-
tude of difafter took it's turn, they found common diftrefs a treacherous bond of faith and
friendfhip.

The greateft fkill conducting the greateft military apparatus has been employed; but it
has been worfe than ufelefsly employed,
through the falfe policy of the war. The operations of the field fuffered by the errors of the
Cabinet. If the fame fpirit continues when
peace is made, the peace will fix and perpetuate
all the errors of the war; becaufe it will be
made upon the fame falfe principle. What
has been loft in the field, in the field may be
regained. An arrangement of peace in it's nature is a permanent fettlement; it is the effect
of

of counfel and deliberation, and not of for-
tuitous events. If built upon a bafis fundamentally erroneous, it can only be retrieved
by fome of thofe unforefeen difpofitions, which
the all-wife but myfterious Governor of the
World, fometimes interpofes, to fnatch nations
from ruin. It would not be pious error, but
mad and impious prefumption for any one to
truft in an unknown order of difpenfations, in
defiance of the rules of prudence, which are
formed upon the known march of the ordinary
providence of God.

It was not of that fort of war that I was
amongft the leaft confiderable, but amongft the
moft zealous advifers ; and it is not by the fort
of peace now talked of, that I wifh it concluded.
It would anfwer no great purpofe to enter into
the particular errours of the war. The whole has
been but one errour. It was but nominally a
war of alliance. As the combined powers purfued it, there was nothing to hold an alliance together. There could be no tie of
honour, in a fociety for pillage. There could be
no tie of a common *intereft* where the object did
not offer fuch a divifion amongft the parties, as
could well give them a warm concern in the
gains of each other, or could indeed form fuch
a body of equivalents, as might make one of
them

them willing to abandon a separate object of
his ambition for the justification of any other
member of the alliance. The partition of Poland
offered an object of spoil in which the parties
might agree. They were circumjacent; and
each might take a portion convenient to his own
territory. They might dispute about the value
of their several shares, but the contiguity to
each of the demandants always furnished the
means of an adjustment. Though hereafter the
world will have cause to rue this iniquitous
measure, and they most who were most concerned in it, for the moment, there was wherewithal in the object to preserve peace amongst
confederates in wrong. But the spoil of France,
did not afford the same facilities for accommodation. What might satisfy the House of
Austria in a Flemish frontier afforded no equivalent to tempt the cupidity of the King of
Pruffia. What might be defired by Great Britain in the West-Indies, must be coldly and
remotely, if at all, felt as an interest at Vienna;
and it would be felt as something worse than a
negative interest at Madrid. Austria, long poffeffed with unwise and dangerous defigns on
Italy, could not be very much in earnest about
the confervation of the old patrimony of the
House of Savoy: and Sardinia, who owed to
an Italian force all her means of shutting out
France

France from Italy, of which fhe has been fuppofed to hold the key, would not purchafe the
means of ftrength upon one fide by yielding it
on the other. She would not readily give the poffeffion of Novara for the hope of Savoy. No
continental Power was willing to lofe any of
it's continental objects for the encreafe of the
naval power of Great Britain; and Great Britain would not give up any of the objects fhe
fought for as the means of an encreafe to her naval power, to further their aggrandizement.

The moment this war came to be confidered
as a war merely of profit, the actual circumftances are fuch, that it never could become
really a war of alliance. Nor can the peace be a
peace of alliance, until things are put upon their
right bottom.

I don't find it denied, that when a treaty is
entered into for peace, a demand will be made
on the Regicides to furrender a great part of
their conquefts on the Continent. Will they,
in the prefent ftate of the war, make that furrender without an equivalent? This continental
ceffion muft of courfe be made in favour of that
party in the alliance, that has fuffered loffes.
That party has nothing to furnifh towards an
equivalent. What equivalent, for inftance, has
Holland

Holland to offer, who has loft her all? What equivalent can come from the Emperor, every part of whofe territories contiguous to France, is already within the pale of the Regicide domination? What equivalent has Sardinia to offer for Savoy and for Nice, I may fay for her whole being? What has fhe taken from the faction of France? She has loft very near her all; and fhe has gained nothing. What equivalent has Spain to give? Alas! fhe has already paid for her own ranfom the fund of equivalent, and a dreadful equivalent it is, to England and to herfelf. But I put Spain out of the queftion. She is a province of the Jacobin Empire, and fhe muft make peace or war according to the orders fhe receives from the Directory of Affaffins. In effect and fubftance, her Crown is a fief of Regicide.

Whence then can the compenfation be demanded? Undoubtedly from that power which alone has made fome conquefts. That power is, England. Will the allies then give away their antient patrimony, that England may keep Iflands in the Weft-Indies? They never can protract the war in good earneft for that object; nor can they act in concert with us, in our refufal, to grant any thing towards their redemption. In that cafe we are thus fituated. Either we muft give Europe, bound hand and foot to France;

or

or we muſt quit the Weſt Indies without any
one object, great or ſmall, towards indemnity
and ſecurity. I repeat it without any advantage
whatever: becauſe, ſuppoſing that our conqueſt
could comprize all that France ever poſſeſſed
in the tropical America, it never can amount in
any fair eſtimation to a fair equivalent for Holland, for the Auſtrian Netherlands, for the
lower Germany, that is for the whole antient
kingdom or circle of Burgundy, now under the
yoke of Regicide, to ſay nothing of almoſt all
Italy under the ſame barbarous domination.
If we treat in the preſent ſituation of things, we
have nothing in our hands that can redeem
Europe. Nor is the Emperor, as I have ob-
ſerved; more rich in the fund of equivalents.

If we look to our ſtock in the Eaſtern world,
our moſt valuable and ſyſtematick acquiſitions
are made in that quarter. Is it from France
they are made? France has but one or two con-
temptible factories, ſubſiſting by the offal of
the private fortunes of Engliſh individuals ro
ſupport them, in any part of India. I look on
the taking of the Cape of Good Hope as the
ſecuring of a poſt of great moment. It does
honour to thoſe who planned, and to thoſe who
executed that enterprize: but I ſpeak of it always as compararively good; as good as any

X   thing

thing can be in a fcheme of war that repels us
from a center, and employs all our forces where
nothing can be finally decifive.   But giving, as
I freely give, every poffible credit to thefe eaftern
conquefts, I afk one queftion, on whom are
they made?   It is evident, that if we can keep
our eaftern conquefts, we keep them 'not at the
expence of France, but at the expence of Holland our *ally*; of Holland the immediate caufe
of the war, the nation whom we had un-
dertaken to protect, and not of the Republic
which it was our bufinefs to deftroy.   If we return the African and the Afiatick conquefts, we
put them into the hands of a nominal State, (to
that Holland is reduced) unable to retain them;
and which will virtually leave them under the
direction of France.   If we withhold them,
Holland declines ftill more as a State; and fhe
lofes fo much carrying trade and that means of
keeping up the fmall degree of naval power fhe
holds; for which policy, and not for any commercial gain, fhe maintains the Cape, or any
fettlement beyond it.   In that cafe, refentment,
faction, and even neceffity will throw her more
and more into the power of the new mifchievous
Republick.   But on the probable ftate of Holland, I fhall fay more, when in this correfpondence I come to talk over with you the ftate in
                                                which

which any fort of Jacobin peace will leave all
Europe.

So far as to the Eaft Indies.

As to the Weft Indies, indeed as to either, if
we look for matter of exchange in order to ranfom Europe, it is eafy to fhew that we have
taken a terribly roundabout road.   I cannot
conceive, even if, for the fake of holding
conquefts there, we fhould refufe to redeem
Holland, and the Auftrian Netherlands, and the
hither Germany, that Spain, merely as fhe is
Spain, (and forgetting that the Regicide Ambaffador governs at Madrid) will fee with perfect fatisfaction, Great Britain fole miftrefs of
the Ifles.   In truth it appears to me, that, when
we come to balance our account, we fhall find
in the propofed peace only the pure, fimple, and
unendowed charms of Jacobin amity.   We fhall
have the fatisfaction of knowing, that no blood
or treafure has been fpared by the allies for fupport of the Regicide fyftem.   We fhall reflect
at leifure on one great truth, that it was ten
times more eafy totally to deftroy the fyftem itfelf, than when eftablifhed, it would be to re-
duce it's power---and that this Republick, moft
formidable abroad, was, of all things, the weakeft at home ;   That her frontier was terrible---

X 2   her

her interior feeble—that it was matter of choice to attack her where fhe is invincible; and to fpare her where fhe was ready to diffolve by her own internal diforders. We fhall reflect, that our plan was good neither for offence nor defence.

My dear Friend, I hold it impoffible that thefe confiderations fhould have efcaped the Statefmen on both fides of the water, and on both fides of the houfe of Commons. How a queftion of peace can be difcuffed without having them in view, I cannot imagine. If you or others fee a way out of thefe difficulties I am happy. I fee indeed a fund from whence equivalents will be propofed. I fee it. But I cannot juft now touch it. It is a queftion of high moment. It opens another Iliad of woes to Europe.

Such is the time propofed for making *a common political peace*, to which no one circumftance is propitious. As to the grand principle of the peace; it is left, as if by common confent, wholly out of the queftion.

Viewing things in this light, I have frequently funk into a degree of defpondency and dejection hardly to be defcribed: yet out of the profoundeft

foundeſt depths of this deſpair, an impulſe
which I have in vain endeavoured to reſiſt,
has urged me to raiſe one feeble cry againſt
this unfortunate coalition which is formed at
home, in order to make a coalition with France,
ſubverſive of the whole ancient order of the
world. No diſaſter of war, no calamity of ſeaſon
could ever ſtrike me with half the horror which
I felt from what is introduced to us by this
junction of parties, under the ſoothing name of
peace. We are apt to ſpeak of a low and pu-
ſillanimous ſpirit as the ordinary cauſe by which
dubious wars terminate in humiliating treaties.
It is here the direct contrary. I am perfectly
aſtoniſhed at the boldneſs of character, at the
intrepidity of mind, the firmneſs of nerve, in
thoſe who are able with deliberation to face the
perils of Jacobin fraternity.

This fraternity is indeed ſo terrible in it's
nature, and in it's manifeſt conſequences, that
there is no way of quieting our apprehenſions
about it, but by totally putting it out of ſight,
by ſubſtituting for it, through a ſort of periphra-
ſis, ſomething of an ambiguous quality, and
deſcribing ſuch a connection under the terms of
" *the uſual relations of peace and amity;*" By this
means the propoſed fraternity is huſtled in the
crowd of thoſe treaties, which imply no change
in

in the public law of Europe, and which do not
upon fyftem affect the interior condition of nations. It is confounded with thofe conventions
in which matters of difpute among fovereign
powers are compromifed, by the taking off a duty
more or lefs, by the furrender of a frontier town,
or a difputed diftrict on the one fide or the other;
by pactions in which the pretenfions of families
are fettled, (as by a conveyancer, making family
fubftitutions and fucceffions) without any alte-
ration in the laws, manners, religion, privileges
and cuftoms of the cities or territories which
are the fubject of fuch arrangements.

All this body of old conventions, compofing
the vaft and voluminous collection called the
corps diplomatique, forms the code or ftatute law,
as the methodized reafonings of the great pub-
licifts and jurifts form the digeft and jurifprudence, of the Chriftian world. In thefe trea-
fures are to be found the *ufual* relations of peace
and amity in civilized Europe; and there the
relations of ancient France were to be found
amongft the reft.

The prefent fyftem in France is not the ancient France. It is not the ancient France with
ordinary ambition and ordinary means. It is not
a new power of an old kind. It is a new power of
a new

a new fpecies. When fuch a queftionable fhape
is to be admitted for the firft time into the bro-
therhood of Chriftendom, it is not a mere matter
of idle curiofity to confider how far it is in it's nature alliable with the reft, or whether " the relations of peace and amity" with this new State
are likely to be of the fame nature with the
ufual relations of the States of Europe.

The Revolution in France had the relation
of France to other nations as one of it's principal objects. The changes made by that Revolution were not the better to accommodate her
to the old and ufual relations, but to produce
new ones. The Revolution was made, not to
make France free, but to make her formidable; not to make her a neighbour, but a miftrefs; not to make her more obfervant of laws,
but to put her in a condition to impofe them.
To make France truly formidable it was neceffary that France fhould be new-modelled. They
who have not followed the train of the late proceedings, have been led by deceitful reprefenta-
tions (which deceit made a part in the plan) to
conceive that this totally new model of a ftate
in which nothing efcaped a change, was made
with a view to it's internal relations only.

In

In the Revolution of France two forts of men were principally concerned in giving a character and determination to it's purfuits ; the philofophers and the politicians. They took different ways, but they met in the fame end. The philofophers had one predominant object, which they purfued with a fanatical fury, that is, the utter extirpation of religion. To that every queftion of empire was fubordinate. They had rather domineer in a parifh of Atheifts, than rule over a Chriftian world. Their temporal ambition was wholly fubfervient to their profelytizing fpirit, in which they were not exceeded by Mahomet himfelf.

They who have made but fuperficial ftudies in the Natural Hiftory of the human mind, have been taught to look on religious opinions as the only caufe of enthufiaftick zeal, and fectarian propagation. But there is no doctrine whatever, on which men can warm, that is not capable of the very fame effect. The focial nature of man impels him to propagate his principles, as much as phyfical impulfes urge him to propagate his kind. The paffions give zeal and vehemence. The underftanding beftows defign and fyftem. The whole man moves under the difcipline of his opinions. Religion is among the moft powerful caufes of enthufiafm. When

any

any thing concerning it becomes an object of much meditation, it cannot be indifferent to the mind. They who do not love religion, hate it. The rebels to God perfectly abhor the Author of their being. They hate him " with all their " heart, with all their mind, with all their foul, " and with all their ftrength." He never prefents himfelf to their thoughts, but to menace and alarm them. They cannot ftrike the Sun out of Heaven, but they are able to raife a fmouldering fmoke that obfcures him from their own eyes. Not being able to revenge themfelves on God, they have a delight in vicarioufly defacing, degrading, torturing, and tearing in pieces his image in man. Let no one judge of them by what he has conceived of them, when they were not incorporated, and had no lead. They were then only paffengers in a common vehicle. They were then carried along with the general motion of religion in the community, and without being aware of it, partook of it's influence. In that fituation, at worft their nature was left free to counterwork their principles. They defpaired of giving any very general currency to their opinions. They confidered them as a referved privilege for the chofen few. But when the poffibility of dominion, lead, and propagation prefented themfelves, and that the ambition, which before had fo often made them hy-

Y   pocrites,

pocrites, might rather gain than lose by a daring avowal of their sentiments, then the nature of this infernal spirit, which has " evil for it's good" appeared in it's full perfection. Nothing indeed but the possession of some power can with any certainty discover, what at the bottom is the true character of any man. Without reading the speeches of Vergniaux, Français of Nantz, Isnard, and some others of that sort, it would not be easy to conceive the passion, rancour, and malice of their tongues and hearts They worked themselves up to a perfect phrenzy against religion and all it's professors. They tore the reputation of the Clergy to pieces by their infuriated declamations and invectives, before they lacerated their bodies by their massacres. This fanatical atheism left out, we omit the principal feature in the French Revolution, and a principal consideration with regard to the effects to be expected from a peace with it.

The other sort of men were the politicians, To them who had little or not at all reflected on the subject, religion was in itself no object of love or hatred. They disbelieved it, and that was all. Neutral with regard to that object, they took the side which in the present state of things might best answer their purposes. They soon found that they could not do without the philosophers ;

fophers; and the philofophers foon made them
fenfible, that the deftruction of religion was to
fupply them with means of conqueft firft at
home, and then abroad. The philofophers
were the active internal agitators, and fupplied the fpirit and principles : the fecond
gave the practical direction. Sometimes the one
predominated in the compofition, fometimes
the other. The only difference between them
was in the neceffity of concealing the general defign for a time, and in their dealing with foreign
nations ; the fanaticks going ftrait forward and
openly, the politici ns by the furer mode of
zigzag. In the' courfe of events this, among
other caufes, produced fierce and bloody con-
tentions between them. But at the bottom
they thoroughly agreed in all the objects of ambition and irreligion, and fubftantially in all the
means of promoting thefe ends.

Without queftion, to bring about the unexampled event of the French revolution, the
concurrence of a very great number of views
and paffi as was neceffary. In that ftupen-
dous work, no one principle by which the human mind may have it's faculties at once in-
vigorated and depraved, was left unemployed:
but I can fpeak it to a certainty, and fupport
it by undoubted proofs, that the ruling prin-

ciple

ciple of thofe who acted in the Revolution *as
ftatefmen*, had the exterior aggrandizement of
France as their ultimate end in the moft minute
part of the internal changes that were made.
We, who of late years, have been drawn from an
attention to foreign affairs by the importance of
our domeftic difcuffions, cannot eafily form a
conception of the general eagernefs of the active
and energetick part of the French nation itfelf,
the moft active and energetick of all nations previous to it's revolution, upon that fubject. I am
convinced that the foreign fpeculators in France,
under the old Government, were twenty to
one of the fame defcription then or now in
England; and few of that defcription there were,
who did not emuloufly let forward the Revolution. The whole offi ial fyftem, particularly in
the diplomatic part, the regulars, the irregulars,
down to the clerks in office, (a corps, without
all comparifon, more numerous than the fame
amongft us) co-operated in it. All the intriguers in foreign politicks, all the fpies, all
the intelligencers, actually or late in function,
all the candidates for that fort of employment,
acted folely upon that principle.

On that fyftem of aggrandizement there
was but one mind : but two violent factions
arofe about the means. The firft wifhed
France,

France, diverted from the politicks of the
continent, to attend folely to her marine,
to feed it by an encreafe of commerce, and
thereby to overpower England on her own
element. They contended, that if England
were difabled, the Powers on the continent
would fall into their proper fubordination; that
it was England which deranged the whole continental fyftem of Europe. The others, who were
by far the more numerous, though not the moft
outwardly prevalent at Court, confidered this
plan for France as contrary to her genius, her
fituation, and her natural means. They agreed
as to the ultimate object, the reduction of
the Britifh power, and if poffible, it's naval
power; but they confidered an afcendancy on
the continent as a neceffary preliminary to that
undertaking. They argued, that the proceedings of England herfelf had proved the foundnefs of this policy. That her greateft and ableft
Statefmen had not confidered the fupport of a
continental balance againft France as a devia-
tion from the principle of her naval power, but
as one of the moft effectual modes of carrying
it into effect. That fuch had been her policy ever fince the Revolution; during which period the naval ftrength of Great Britain had
gone on encreafing in the direct ratio of
her interference in the politicks of the continent.

nent. With much ftronger reafon ought the politicks of France to take the fame direction; as well for purfuing objects which her fituation would dictate to her, though England had no exiftence, as for counteracting the politicks of that nation; to France continental politicks are primary; they looked on them only of fecondary confideration to England, and however neceffary, but as means neceffary to an end.

What is truly aftonifhing, the partizans of thofe two oppofite fyftems were at once prevalent, and at once employed, and in the very fame tranfactions, the one oftenfibly, the other fecretly, during the latter part of the reign of Lewis XV. Nor was there one Court in which an Ambaffador refided on the part of the Minifters, in which another as a fpy on him did not alfo refide on the part of the King They who purfued the fcheme for keeping peace on the continent, and particularly with Auftria, acting officially and publickly, the other faction counteracting and oppofing them Thefe private agents were continually going from their function to the Baftille, and from the Baftille to employment, and favour again. An inextricable cabal was formed, fome of perfons of rank, others of fubordinates. But by this

means

means the, corps of politicians was augmented
in number, and the whole formed a body of
active, adventuring, ambitious, difcontented
people, defpifing the regular Miniftry, defpifing the Courts at which they were employed,
defpifing the Court which employed them.

The unfortunate Louis the Sixteenth * was
not the firft caufe of the evil by which he fuffered. He came to it, as to a fort of inheritance,
by the falfe politicks of his immediate predecef-

* It may be right to do juftice to Louis XVI. He did
what he could to deftroy the double diplomacy of France.
He had all the fecret correfpondence burnt, except one
piece, which was called, *Conjectures ra'fonnées fur la Situation
de la France dans le Syfteme Politique de l'Europe*; a work executed by M. Favier, under the direction of Count Broglie.
A fingle copy of this was faid to have been found in the Cabinet of Louis XVI. It was publifhed with fome fubfequent
ftate papers of Vergennes, Turgot, and others, as, " A new
Benefit of the Revolution ;" and the advertifement to the
publication ends with the following words. " *Il fera facile
de fe convaincre, qu*' Y COMPRIS MEME LA REVOLUTION, *en*
grande partie, ON TROUVE DANS CES MEMOIRES ET SES CON-
JECTURES LE GERME DE TOUT CE QU' ARRIVA AUJOURD'-
HUI, *& qu'on ne peut pas fans les avoir lus, être bien au fait des
intérêts, & même des vues actuelles des diverfes puiffances de
l'Europe.*" The book is entitled, *Politique de tous les Cabinets
de l'Europe pendant les regnes de Louis* XV. *& Louis* XVI.
It is altogether very curious, and worth reading.

for

for. This fyftem of dark and perplexed intrigue had come to it's perfection before he came.
to the throne: and even then the Revolution
ftrongly operated in all it's caufes.

There was no point on which the difcontented
diplomatic politicians fo bitterly arraigned their
Cabinet, as for the decay of French influence in all others. From quarrelling with
the Court, they began to complain of Monarchy itfelf; as a fyftem of Government too
variable for any regular plan of national aggrandizement. They obferved, that in that
fort of regimen too much depended on the
perfonal character of the Prince; that the viciffitudes produced by the fucceffion of Princes
of a different character, and even the viciffitudes
produced in the fame man, by the different views
and inclinations belonging to youth, manhood,
and age, difturbed and diftracted the policy of
a country made by nature for extenfive empire,
or what was ftill more to their tafte, for that
fort of general over-ruling influence which prepared empire or fupplied the place of it. They
had continually in their hands the obfervations
of *Machiavel* on *Livy*. They had *Montefquieu's
Grandeur & Décadence des Romains* as a manual;
and they compared with mortification the fyf-
tematic proceedings of a Roman fenate with the
fluctuations

fluctuations of a Monarchy. They observed, the very small additions of territory which all the power of France, actuated by all the ambition of France, had acquired in two centuries. The Romans had frequently acquired more in a single year. They severely and in every part of it criticised the reign of Louis the XIVth, whose irregular and desultory ambition had more provoked than endangered Europe. Indeed, they who will be at the pains of seriously considering the history of that period will see, that those French politicians had some reason. They who will not take the trouble of reviewing it through all it's wars and all it's negociations, will consult the short but judicious criticism of the Marquis de Montalambert on that subject. It may be read separately from his ingenious system of fortification and military defence, on the practical merit of which I am unable to form a judgment.

The diplomatick politicians of whom I speak, and who formed by far the majority in that class, made disadvantageous comparisons even between their more legal and formalising Monarchy, and the monarchies of other states, as a system of power and influence. They observed, that France not only lost ground herself, but through the languor and unsteadiness of her pur-

Z   suits,

fuits, and from her aiming through commerce at
naval force which fhe never could attain without
lofing more on one fide than fhe could gain on
the other, three great powers, each of them (as
military ftates) capable of balancing her, had
grown up on the continent. Ruffia and Pruffia
had been created almoft-within memory; and
Auftria, though not a new power, and even cur-
tailed in territory, was by the very collifion in
which fhe loft that territory, greatly improved
in her military difcipline and force. During the reign of Maria Therefa the interior
œconomy of the country was made more to cor-
refpond with the fupport of great armies than
formerly it had been. As to Pruffia, a merely
military power, they obferved that one war had
enriched her with as confiderable a conqueft as
France had acquired in centuries. Ruffia had
broken the Turkifh power by which Auftria
might be, as formerly fhe had been, balanced
in favour of France. They felt it with pain,
that the two northern powers of Sweden and
Denmark were in general under the fway of
Ruffia; or that at beft, France kept up a very
doubtful conflict, with many fluctuations of
fortune, and at an enormous expence in Sweden. In Holland, the French party feemed,
if not extinguifhed, at leaft utterly obfcured,
and kept under by a Stadtholder, fometimes
leaning for fupport on Great Britain, fometimes

on

on Pruffia, fometimes on both, never on France. Even the fpreading of the Bourbon family had become merely a family accommodation; and had little effect on the national politicks. This alliance, they faid, extinguished Spain by deftroying all it's energy, without adding any thing to the real power of France in the acceffion of the forces of it's great rival. In Italy, the fame family accommodation, the fame national infignificance were equally vifible. What cure for the radical weaknefs of the French Monarchy, to which all the means which wit could devife, or nature and fortune could beftow, towards univerfal empire, was not of force to give life, or vigour, or confiftency,—but in a republick? Out the word came; and it never went back.

Whether they reafoned right or wrong, or that there was fome mixture of right and wrong in their reafoning, I am fure, that in this manner they felt and reafoned. The different effects of a great military and ambitious republick, and of a monarchy of the fame defcription were conftantly in their mouths. The principle was ready to operate when opportunities fhould offer, which few of them indeed forefaw in the extent in which they were afterwards prefented; but thefe opportunities, in fome degree or other, they all ardently wifhed for.

Z 2

When

When I was in Paris in 1773, the treaty of 1756 between Auftria and France was deplored as a national calamity; becaufe it united France in friendfhip with a Power, at whofe expence alone they could hope any continental aggrandizement. When the firft partition of Poland was made, in which France had no fhare, and which had farther aggrandized every one of the three Powers of which they were moft jealous, I found them in a perfect phrenzy of rage and indignation: Not that they were hurt at the fhocking and uncoloured violence and injuftice of that partition, but at the debility, improvidence, and want of activity in their Government, in not preventing it as a means of aggrandizement to their rivals, or in not contriving, by exchanges of fome kind or other, to obtain their fhare of advantage from that robbery.

In that or nearly in that ftate of things and of opinions, came the Auftrian match; which promifed to draw the knot, as afterwards in effect it did, ftill more clofely between the old rival houfes. This added exceedingly to their hatred and contempt of their monarchy. It was for this reafon that the late glorious Queen, who on all accounts was formed to produce general love and admiration, and whofe life was as mild and beneficent as her death was beyond example great and heroic, be-

came

came fo very foon and fo very much the object of an implacable rancour, never to be extinguifhed but in her blood. When I wrote my letter in anfwer to M. de Menonville, in the beginning of January, 1791, I had good reafon for thinking that this defcription of revolutionifts did not fo early nor fo fteadily point their murderous defigns at the martyr King as at the Royal Heroine. It was accident, and the momentary depreffion of that part of the faction, that gave to the hufband the happy priority in death.

From this their reftlefs defire of an over-ruling influence, they bent a very great part of their defigns and efforts to revive the old French party, which was a democratick party in Holland, and to make a revolution there. They were happy at the troubles which the fingular imprudence of Jofeph the Second had ftirred up in the Auftrian Netherlands. They rejoiced, when they faw him irritate his fubjects, profefs philofophy, fend away the Dutch garrifons, and difmantle his fortifications. As to Holland, they never forgave either the King or the Miniftry, for fuffering that object, which they juftly looked on as principal in their defign of reducing the power of England, to efcape out of their hands. This was the true fecret of the commercial treaty, made, on their part, againft all

the

the old rules and principles of commerce, with a view of diverting the Englifh nation, by a pur- fuit of immediate profit, from an attention to the progrefs of France in it's defigns upon that Republic. The fyftem of the œconomifts, which led to the general opening of commerce, facili- tated that treaty, but did not produce it. They were in defpair when they found that by the vigour of Mr. Pitt, fupported in this point by Mr. Fox and the oppofition, the objeét, to which they had facrificed their manufaétures, was loft to their ambition. This eager de- fire of raifing France from the condition into which fhe had fallen, as they conceived, from her monarchical imbecillity, had been the main fpring of their precedent interference in that un- happy American quarrel, the bad effeéts of which to this nation have not, as yet, fully dif- clofed themfelves.

Thefe fentiments had been long lurking in their breafts, though their views were only dif- covered now and then, in heat and as by efcapes; but on this occafion they exploded fuddenly. They were profeffed with oftentation, and pro- pagated with zeal. Thefe fentiments were not produced, as fome think, by their American alliance. The American alliance was produced by their republican principles and republican
policy

policy. This new relation undoubtedly did much. The difcourfes and cabals that it produced, the intercourfe that it eftablifhed, and above all, the example, which made it feem practicable to eftablifh a Republick in a great extent of country, finifhed the work, and gave to that part of the Revolutionary faction a degree of ftrength, which required other energics than the late King poffefled, to refift, or even to reftrain. It fpread every where; but it was no where more prevalentthan in the heart of the Court. The palace of Verfailles, by it's language, feemed a forum of democracy. To have pointed out to moft of thofe politicians, from their difpofitions and movements, what has fince happened, the fall of their own Monarchy, of their own Laws, of their own Religion, would have been to furnifh a motive the more for pufhing forward a fyftem on which they confidered all thefe things as incumbrances. Such in truth they were. And we have feen them fucceed not only in the deftruction of their monarchy; but in all the objects of ambition that they propofed from that deftruction.

When I contemplate the fcheme on which France is formed, and when I compare it with thefe fyftems, with which it is, and ever muft be in conflict, thofe things which feem as defects in her polity, are the very things which make me tremble. The States of the Chriftian World have grown up to their prefent magnitude in a great length of time, and by a great variety of accidents. They have been improved to what we fee them with greater or lefs degrees of felicity and fkill. Not one of them has been formed upon a regular plan or with any unity of defign. As their Conftitutions are not fyftematical, they have not been directed to any *peculiar* end, eminently diftinguifhed, and fuperfeding every other. The objects which they embrace are of the greateft poffible variety, and have become in a manner infinite. In all thefe old countries the ftate has been made to the people, and not the people conformed to the ftate. Every ftate has purfued, not only every fort of focial advantage, but it has cultivated the welfare of every individual. His wants, his wifhes, even his taftes have been confulted. This comprehenfive fcheme, virtually produced a degree of perfonal liberty in forms the moft adverfe to it. That liberty was found, under monarchies ftiled abfolute, in a degree unknown to the ancient commonwealths. From hence the powers of all our modern ftates, meet in all their movements, with fome obftruction. It is therefore no wonder, that when thefe ftates are to be confidered as machines to operate for fome one great end, that this diffipated and balanced force is not eafily concentred, or made to bear with the whole nation upon one point.

The Britifh State is, without queftion, that which purfues the greateft variety of ends,

and is the leaft difpofed to facrifice any one of
them to another, or to the whole. It aims at
taking in the entire circle of human defires, and
fecuring for them their fair enjoyment. Our legiflature has been ever clofely connected, in it's moft
efficient part, with individual feeling and individual intereft. Perfonal liberty, the moft lively of
thefe feelings and the moft important of thefe interefts, which in other European countries has
rather arifen from the fyftem of manners and the
habitudes of life, than from the laws of the ftate, (in
which it flourifhed more from neglect than attention) in England, has been a direct object of
Government.

On this principle England would be the weakeft
power in the whole fyftem. Fortunately, however, the great riches of this kingdom, arifing
from a vaiety of caufes, and the difpofition of
the people, which is as great to fpend as to accu-
mulate, has eafily afforded a difpofeable furplus that
gives a mighty momentum to the ftate. This difficulty, with thefe advantages to overcome it, has
called forth the talents of the Englifh financiers,
who, by the furplus of induftry poured out by pro-
digality, have outdone every thing which has been
accomplifhed in other nations. The prefent Minifter has outdone his predeceffors; and as a
Minifter of revenue, is far above my power of
praife. But ftill there are cafes in which Eng-

land

land feels more than feveral others, (though they all feel) the perplexity of an inmenfe body of balanced advantages, and of individual demands, and of fome irregularity in the whole mafs.

France differs effentially from all thofe Governments which are formed without fyftem, which exift by habit, and which are confufed with the multitude, and with the complexity of their purfuits. What now ftands as Government in France is ftruck out at a heat. The defign is wicked, immoral, impious, oppreffive; but it is fpirited and daring; it is fyftematick; it is fimple in it's principle; it has unity and confiftency in perfection. In that country entirely to cut off a branch of commerce, to extinguifh a manufacture, to deftroy the circulation of money, to violate credit, to fufpend the courfe of argriculture, even to burn a city, or to lay wafte a province of their own, does not coft them a moment's anxiety. To them, the will, the wifh, the want, the liberty, the toil, the blood of individuals is as nothing. Individuality is left out of their fcheme of Government. The ftate is all in all. Every thing is referred to the production of force; afterwards every thing is trufted to the ufe of it. It is military in it's principle, in it's maxims, in it's fpirit, and in all it's movements. The ftate has dominion and conqueft for it's fole objects; dominion over minds by profelytifm, over bodies by arms.

Thus

Thus conftituted with an immenfe body of natural means, which are leffened in their amount
only to be increafed in their effect, France has,
fince the accomplifhment of the Revolution, a
complete unity in it's direction. It has deftroyed
every refource of the State, which depends upon
opinion and the good-will of individuals. The
riches of convention difappear. The advantages
of nature in fome meafure remain; even thefe, I
admit, are aftonifhingly leffened; the command
over what remains is complete and abfolute.
We go about afking when affignats will expire,
and we laugh at the laft price of them. But what
fignifies the fate of thofe tickets of defpotifm?
The defpotifm will find defpotick means of fupply. They have found the fhort cut to the productions of Nature, while others in purfuit of
them, are obliged to wind through the labyrinth
of a very intricate ftate of fociety. They feize
upon the fruit of the labour; they feize upon
the labourer himfelf. Were France but half of
what it is in population, in compactnefs, in applica-
bility of it's force, fituated as it is, and being what it is,
it would be too ftrong for moft of the States of Europe, conftituted as they are, and proceeding as they
proceed. Would it be wife to eftimate what the
world of Europe, as well as the world of Afia, had to
dread from Jinghiz Khân, upon a contemplation
of the refources of the cold and barren fpot in the
remoteft Tartary, from whence firft iffued that

A a 2   fcourge

scourge of the human race ? Ought we to judge from the excise and stamp duties of the rocks, or from the paper circulation of the sands of Arabia, the power by which Mahomet and his tribes laid hold at once on the two most powerful Empires of the world ; beat one of them totally to the ground, broke to pieces the other, and, in not much longer space of time than I have lived, overturned governments, laws, manners, religion, and extended an empire from the Indus to the Pyrennees.

Material resources never have supplied, nor ever can supply the want of unity in design and constancy in pursuit. But unity in design, and perseverance, and boldness in pursuit, have never wanted resources, and never will. We have not considered as we ought the dreadful energy of a State, in which the property has nothing to do with the Government. Reflect, my dear Sir, reflect again and again on a Government, in which the property is in complete subjection, and where nothing rules but the mind of desperate men. The condition of a commonwealth not governed by it's property was a combination of things, which the learned and ingenious speculator Harrington, who has tossed about society into all forms, never could imagine to be possible. We have seen it ; the world has felt it ; and if the world will shut their eyes to this state of things, they will feel it more. The Rulers there have found their resources in crimes. The

discovery

difcovery is dreadful: the mine exhauftlefs. T\ have every thing to gain, and they have nothing ᴗ lofe. . They have a boundlefs inheritance in hope : and there is no medium for them, betwixt the higheft elevation, and death with infamy. Never can they who from the miferable fervitude of the defk have been raifed to Empire, again fubmit to the bondage of a ftarving bureau, or the profit of copying mufic, or writing plaidoyers by the fheet. It has made me often fmile in bitternefs, when I have heard talk of an indemnity to fuch men, pro-vided they returned to their allegiance.

From all this, what is my inference? It is, that this new fyftem of robbery in France, cannot be rendered fafe by any art; that it *muft* be deftroyed, or that it will deftroy all Europe; that to deftroy that enemy, by fome means or other, the force op-pofed to it fhould be made to bear fome analogy and refemblance to the force and fpirit which that fyftem exerts; that war ought to be made againft it, in its vulnerable parts. Thefe are my infe-rences. In one word, with this Republick nothing independent can co-exift. The errors of Louis the XVIth. were more pardonable to prudence, than any of thofe of the fame kind into which the Allied Courts may fall. They have the benefit of his dreadful example.

The unhappy Louis XVI. was a man of the beft
intentions

intentions that probably ever reigned. He was by
no means deficient in talents. He had a most
laudable defire to fupply by general reading, and
even by the acquifition of elemental knowledge,
an education in all points originally defective ; but
nobody told him (and it was no wonder he fhould
not himfelf divine it) that the world of which he
read, and the world in which he lived, were no
longer the fame. Defirous of doing every thing
for the beft, fearful of cabal, diftrufting his
own judgment, he fought his Minifters of all kinds
upon public teftimony. But as Courts are the
field for caballers, the publick is the theatre for
mountebanks and impoftors. The cure for both
thofe evils is in the difcernment of the Prince.
But an accurate and penetrating difcernment is
what in a young Prince could not be looked for.

His conduct in it's principle was not unwife ; but,
like moft other of his well-meant defigns, it failed
in his hands. It failed partly from mere ill fortune,
to which fpeculators are rarely pleafed to affign that
very large fhare to which fhe is juftly entitled in
all human affairs. The failure, perhaps, in part
was owing to his fuffering his fyftem to be vitiated
and difturbed by thofe intrigues, which it is, hu-
manly fpeaking, impoffible wholly to prevent in
Courts, or indeed under any form of Government.
However, with thefe aberrations, he gave himfelf
over to a fucceffion of the ftatefmen of publick
opinion,

opinion. In other things he thought that he might be a King on the terms of his predeceſſors. He was conſcious of the purity of his heart and the general good tendency of his Government. He flattered himſelf, as moſt men in his ſituation will, that he might conſult his eaſe without danger to his ſafety. It is not at all wonderful that both he and his Miniſters, giving way abundantly in other reſpects to innovation, ſhould take up in policy with the tradition of their monarchy. Under his anceſtors the Monarchy had ſubſiſted, and even been ſtrengthened by the generation or ſupport of Republicks. Firſt, the Swiſs Republicks grew under the guardianſhip of the French Monarchy. The Dutch Republicks were hatched and cheriſhed under the ſame incubation. Afterwards, a republican conſtitution was under it's influence eſtabliſhed in the Empire againſt the pretenſions of it's Chief. Even whilſt the Monarchy of France, by a ſeries of wars and negotiations, and laſtly by the treaties of Weſtphalia, had obtained the eſtabliſhment of the Proteſtants in Germany as a law of the Empire, the ſame Monarchy under Louis the XIIIth, had force enough to deſtroy the republican ſyſtem of the Proteſtants at home.

Louis the XVIth was a diligent reader of hiſtory. But the very lamp of prudence blinded him. The guide of human life led him aſtray. A ſilent revolution in the moral world preceded the political,

cal, and prepared it. It became of more importance than ever what examples were given, and what meatures were adopted. Their caufes no longer lurked in the receffes of cabinets, or in the private confpiracies of the factious. They were no longer to be controlled by the force and influence of the grandees, who formerly had been able to ftir up troubles by their difcontents, and to quiet them by their corruption. The chain of fubordination, even in cabal and fedition, was broken in it's moft important links. It was no longer the great and the populace. Other interefts were formed, other dependencies, other connexions, other communications. The middle claffes had fwelled far beyond their former proportion. Like whatever is the moft effectively rich and great in fociety, thefe claffes became the feat of all the active politicks; and the preponderating weight to decide on them. There were all the energies by which fortune is acquired; there the confequence of their fuccefs. There were all the talents which affert their pretenfions, and are impatient of the place which fettled fociety prefcribes to them. Thefe defcriptions had got between the great and the populace; and the influence on the lower claffes was with them. The fpirit of ambition had taken poffeffion of this clafs as violently as ever it had done of any other. They felt the importance of this fituation. The correfpondence of the monied and the mercantile world, the literary intercourfe of academics, mies; but, above all, the prefs, of which they had in a manner, entire poffeffion, made a kind of electrick communication every where. The prefs, in reality, has made every Government, in it's fpirit, almoft democratick. Without the great, the firft movements in this revolution could not, perhaps, have been given. But the fpirit of ambition, now for the firft time connected with the fpirit of fpeculation, was not to be reftrained at will. There was no longer any means of arrefting a principle in it's courfe. When Louis the XVIth. under the influence of the enemies to Monarchy, meant to found but one Republick, he fet up two. When he meant to take away half the crown of his neighbour, he loft the whole of his own. Louis the XVIth could not with impunity countenance a new Republick: yet between his throne and that dangerous lodgment for an enemy, which he had erected, he had the whole Atlantick for a ditch. He had for an out-work the Englifh nation itfelf, friendly to liberty, adverfe to that mode of it. He was furrounded by a rampart of Monarchies, moft of them allied to him, and generally under his influence. Yet even thus fecured, a Republick erected under his aufpices, and dependent on his power, became fatal to his throne. The very money which he had lent to fupport this Republick, by a good faith, which to him operated as perfidy, was punctually paid to his enemies, and became a refource in the hands of his affaffins.

B b

With this example before their eyes, do any
Ministers in England, do any Ministers in Austria, really flatter themselves, that they can
erect, not on the remote shores of the Atlantick,
but in their view, in their vicinity, in absolute con-
tact with one of them, not a commercial but a
martial Republick—a Republick not of simple
husbandmen or fishermen, but of intriguers, and
of warriors—a Republick of a character the most
restless, the most enterprizing, the most impious,
the most fierce and bloody, the most hypocritical
and perfidious, the most bold and daring that ever
has been seen, or indeed that can be conceived to
exist, without bringing on their own certain ruin?

Such is the Republick to which we are going
to give a place in civilized fellowship. The Republick, which with joint consent we are going to
establish in the center of Europe, in a post that
overlooks and commands every other State, and
which eminently confronts and menaces this kingdom.

You cannot fail to observe, that I speak as if the
allied powers were actually consenting, and not compelled by events to the establishment of this faction
in France. The words have not escaped me. You
will hereafter naturally expect that I should make
them good. But whether in adopting this mea-

commu-

sure we are madly active, or weakly passive, or pu-
sillanimously panick-struck, the effects will be the
same. You may call this faction, which has era-
dicated the monarchy,—expelled the proprietary,
persecuted religion, and trampled upon law*,—you
may call this France if you please: but of
the ancient France nothing remains; but it's
central geography; it's iron frontier; it's spirit of
ambition; it's audacity of enterprise; it's perplexing intrigue. These and these alone remain; and
they remain heightened in their principle and augmented in their means. All the former correctives,
whether of virtue or of weakness, which existed in the
old Monarchy, are gone. No single new corrective
is to be found in the whole body of the new insti-
tutions. How should such a thing be found there,
when every thing has been chosen with care and selection to forward all those ambitious designs and dif-
positions, not to controul them? The whole is a
body of ways and means for the supply of dominion, without one heterogeneous particle in it.

Here I suffer you to breathe, and leave to your
meditation what has occurred to me on the *genius
and character* of the French Revolution. From
having this before us, we may be better able to determine on the first question I proposed, that is, how

---

* See our declaration.

far

far nations, called foreign, are likely to be affected
with the fyftem eftablished within that territory?
I intended to proceed next on the queftion of her facilities, from *the internal ftate of other nations, and
particularly of this,* for obtaining her ends: but I
ought to be aware, that my notions are controvert-
ed.—I mean, therefore, in my next letter, to take
notice of what, in that way, has been recommended to me as the moft deferving of notice. In the
examination of thofe pieces, I fhall have occafion
to difcufs fome others of the topics I have recommended to your attention. You know, that the
Letters which I now fend to the prefs, as well as a
part of what is to follow, have been long fince
written. A circumftance which your partiality
alone could make of importance to you, but which
to the publick is of no importance at all, retarded
their appearance. The late events which prefs
upon us obliged me to make fome few additions;
but no fubftantial change in the matter.

This difcuffion, my Friend, will be long. But
the matter is ferious; and if ever the fate of the
world could be truly faid to depend on a particular
meafure, it is upon this peace. For the prefent,
farewel,

www.ingramcontent.com/pod-product-compliance
Lightning Source LLC
Chambersburg PA
CBHW030843270326
41928CB00007B/1191

* 9 7 8 3 3 3 7 1 0 6 9 8 0 *